THE MANUAL OF FINANCIAL FREEDOM

BUSINESS FOR BEGINNERS

2020

Disclaimer

All erudition supplied in this book is specified for educational and academic purpose only. The author is not in any way in charge of any outcomes that emerge from utilizing this book. Constructive efforts have been made to render information that is both precise and effective; however, the author is not to be held answerable for the accuracy or use/misuse of this information.

Foreword

I will like to thank you for taking the very first step of trusting me and deciding to purchase/read this life-transforming book. Thanks for investing your time and resources on this product.

I can assure you of precise outcomes if you will diligently follow the specific blueprint I lay bare in the information handbook you are currently checking out. It has transformed lives, and I strongly believe it will equally transform your own life too.

All the information I provided in this Do It Yourself piece is easy to absorb and practice.

Table of Contents

EXTRA

CHAPTER ONE

Think Like A Rich

What I will suggest in the first chapters is that, possibly, just maybe, how we think of wealth may hold us back from being wealthy.

If in our heart, we think (even subconsciously) that money is a bad thing and having a lot of it is a bad thing; the possibilities are we might be weakening our own efforts, unknowingly, to get great deals of it.

I am likewise going to get you to look at just how much effort you are prepared to take into earning money. It's a bit like a sport, the more you practice, the better you end up being. Similarly, you can't earn money while slouching. You have to put in some work here, you know. You've also got to understand quite totally what you desire, why you desire it, how you believe you are going to get it, what you are going to make with it after you've got it like that. No one says this is going to be easy .

Rule 1: Anyone Can Be Wealthy, You Just Need to Apply Yourself

The lovely feature of money is that it truly does not discriminate. It does not care what color or race you are, what class you are, what your moms and dads did, or even who you believe you are. Each and every day begins with a fresh start so that no matter what you did yesterday, today starts anew, and you have the very same rights and chances as everyone else would desire. The only thing that can hold you are yourself and your own money fiction. The wealth in the world, each has as much as they take. What else could make sense? There is no way money can understand who is handling it, what their credentials are, what aspirations they have, or what class they come from. Money has no eyes or ears or senses. It is inert, inanimate, impassive. It hasn't a hint. It is there to be utilized and spent, conserved and invested, contested, seduced with or worked for it. It has no discriminatory level, so it can not evaluate whether you are "deserving".

I have enjoyed a lot of wealthy individuals, and the one thing they all have in common is that they have absolutely nothing in common, apart from all being Rules Players, of course. The rich are a varied band of people, the least likely can be packed. And the bad are the ones saying, "No, thank you, not for me, I am not worthy."

That's what we would talk about in this book, challenging your understandings of money and the wealthy. If you have the means to buy a book such as this and live in relative security and convenience in the world, then you too have the power to be rich. And that is Rule 1: anyone can be wealthy, you just have to apply yourself. You have the rights and opportunities as everyone else to take as much as you want.

Understand Your Money Beliefs and Where They are Coming.

We all grow up with cash myths. My cash misconceptions are based on a lot of nonsense like that. Many of us have the following deep-rooted beliefs:

In fact, the love of cash that is expected to be the root of all evil; however, is it a belief of yours?

- Money is filthy.
- I won't be worthy of being abundant.
- Money is only made by the dishonest and greedy.
- Money corrupts.
- You need to not extol cash. Never ever say how much you make, deserve, or paid for something (unless it is a deal).
- Money is the root of all evil.
- You can not have money and be "spiritually exhorted."
- You lose your pals if you get rich.
- You need to work too difficult to get rich
- Joy and money make poor bedfellows.

3

- The more you have, the more you'll desire.
- It is somehow much better to be poor.
- I wasn't implied to be abundant-- if I were, where I would have been by now.
- I'm not the right type to be wealthy.

Have a peek through.

Examine which ones you think. Check which one strikes a chord with you. Now you need to make a bit of that old-fashioned effort. Write out the ones that mean something to you. Include the ones I've missed out on, there will be a couple of.

Now work out on why you have these beliefs. Is it something you have actively thought of, reasoned out, dedicated some research to? Or are they inherited, leftover, chose up along the way?

Get rid of any that you can accept, discard any that just aren't real. And remove any that stand in the way, hold you back, stop you making some cash.

What you ought to be left with is none, absolutely nothing, a blank sheet. Now you can write new beliefs such as :

- Money is OK.
- Wanting money is OKAY.
- I am going to be rich.
- I am prepared to put in the effort.

4

Rich people have none of the problematic money misconceptions we poorer people do have, They have purged them or never had them. We stand a much better possibility of getting there if we too purge them.

Rule 2: Believe That Wealth Is A Reward And Not A Consequeces

The word reward used implies to a bonus or prize but not a mode of renumeration or payment. You stand a much better chance of ending up being rich if you work hard at making money. You need to accept that money is a payment offered to you for clever thinking and effort. The more difficult and smarter you work, the more you will earn. You aren't offered the cash by a committee who analyzes whether you deserve it, whether you have actually been excellent enough. It is a direct effect.

We frequently take a look at someone who has money and makes all sorts of worth judgments about whether they deserve it. All of us do it.

Rule 3: Decide What You Want Money For

There are no right or wrong answers. Making a fortune and lavish it all on cocaine appears, to me, like an absurd thing to do. We all spend on what we believe will please us, make us pleased.

So why do you wish to be wealthy? The answers you provide will tell you an entire lot about your surprise money myths and how you actually see the cash.

Often it's very easy: We have a dream and need the money to meet it. The dream comes. What's your dream?

It might not be that simple. I asked a close acquaintance why she wished to be wealthier recently, and the results were rather revealing. She stated she wished to be "better off" so that she could give her kids more. And in offering them more, they would remain at home longer. And if they remained at home longer, she wouldn't have to deal with possible aging alone. So basically, she wants to be rich to stave off loneliness.

Another associate said he wished to get wealthy so that he might be able to see the world. When questioned further, it likely his adventures were the "escaping" sort where he might be young, complimentary, and single once again.

Is money actually the response for either of these individuals? Is it for you?

When you understand what you want greater wealth for, also believe about alternative methods to meet your needs: I might say, I wish to be rich so that I could pay for medical care for any close family member that may need it. I might purchase some simple medical insurance coverage to cover that instead.

Think about likewise what you do not need more money for. Do you truly require as much as you think?

What do you want money for? It might be too complimentary you from having a job, or it might not even be for yourself but to support causes you think in. And whatever you compose down-- and I do suggest you write it down; it makes it so much more genuine.a lot more real. It is a useful workout to reflect on one day to see if your dream and achievements match.

CHAPTER TWO

Developing Wealth

Ever question how some people have a great deal of money and just keep making a vast number of money, while some individuals battle to make ends satisfy, despite the fact that they keep doing everything they can to make more cash? Or why some individuals always have the cash to buy what they want while others continue to accumulate their financial obligations even though they have a decent job? I'm going to discuss why this occurs and how you can turn into one of those people who is always living life with positive money flow.

Positive Wealth Consciousness

Throughout the years through a research study, interviews, I've discovered that individuals who have an excellent deal of wealth and individuals who preserve a favorable capital have actually established a favorable wealth awareness. Simply because they always have money because they always believe they will have money. As a result, they constantly draw in cash and moneymaking, while at the exact same time, they discover methods to conserve cash and make their money work for them. Now it wasn't constantly by doing this. Not everyone had money to start within in reality, a lot of individuals made their cash and continued to find methods to make more cash.

I keep in mind talking to a buddy, who owns a chain of hotels across the United States and is now expanding into Canada and overseas. He explained he had actually originated from an immigrant family; his daddy worked as an accounting professional and later on opened a store while his mother put herself through school eventually ending up being a nursing sister. However, my point is he didn't have a family that provided him with a million dollars to start his endeavor. Rather he began off working for his father, ultimately took control of the company, bought another, made it a success offered it and purchased another till he got his first hotel just outside Dallas.

I asked him: "Were you ever nervous? Did you ever think of failing? Did you ever have those what-if ideas?" He addressed: "They entered my mind but I dismissed them rather rapidly, I just believed about making it happen and convinced myself that it would take place. After that, I never doubted I would prosper, I simply didn't understand how huge this entire thing would get." In other words, Ivan developed a positive wealth awareness without being aware of what he had actually done, however, he had trained his mind and subconscious to focus only on creating wealth.

Lets define positive wealth consciuosness as a method of believing that you can and will generate income. It involves thinking that it is your right to generate income and create wealth. It needs that you concentrate on all the great things that your wealth can do for you and those around you. If you have wealth, you will assist more individuals, and it means understanding that. It suggests putting your ego aside- not wanting wealth so that you can flaunt and say: "Look at me, I'm rich." Rather it suggests saying: "Yes, I have a lot of wealth which enables me to take care of a lot of people, including my household and all those that I help when I invest my money."

You will invest your money, let's face it , the more you have, the more you will spend.

In order to bring in wealth, you need to very first take a look at where you are now and then create a realistic approach for a couple of months,a year, or more years. Perhaps you are indebted due to the task- intending to have a million dollars in 6 months is not being extremely realistic. Rather your very first priority must be to get and get a job out of debt. If you currently have a job and you want to make more cash then offer yourself some sensible targets for the next 3 months, 6 months, year, and 5 years. Now I understand a few of you will say it's tough to generate the income, I do not know what to do to make more money, I'm in debt and don't understand how to go out. For each issue, there is an option of solution otherwise, we would not have problems. Concentrate on finding an option. Train your mind to focus on the service. Begin to forward messages to your conscious mind for a solution. Do this frequently, and you'll get answers. The money will not fall from the sky, but you will be guided to it. How Do You Train Your Mind? You initially focus on what you desire. Let's state you wish to find a task- you start to proclaim that you know what to do to find a task.

What You Can Do To Attract Wealth

There are a variety of techniques you can employ to attract wealth, regardless of your situation. You have to get your mind to work for you and not versus you. Here's a little exercise you can do. Get a notepad and a pen. Now begin thinking of generating income or enhancing your financial resources. Jot down all the thoughts that come to mind when you think of enhancing your finances or creating wealth. Be sincere – then you will see this list. Keep going until you feel you have had to satisfy. Keep contributing to that list throughout the day. Then when you feel you have got enough - have a look at what you wrote. Highlight the thoughts that are favorable and circle the ideas that are negative. How lots of are you negative? Any negative thought that you have about money or to improve your finances is connected to a belief that you have about money and only works against you. If you believe it's challenging to make more cash, you'll only have problems when it concerns making cash. Why? Due to the fact that your subconscious mind is just going to develop your truth based on your beliefs. If these beliefs are bad or great for you, it doesn't care. It simply acts upon your guidelines, and those guidelines are your beliefs and thoughts. To alter your thoughts and you change your beliefs. Modify your beliefs, and you change your life.

CHAPTER THREE

Guidelines For Getting Wealthy

This is where we will get serious. This is where we start the practical thins and where you need to begin taking a good at your circumstance, doing some planning, and taking some action.

You getting rich means being very sincere with yourself and being prepared to invest your time and efforts into the mission for greater prosperity. A number of the Rules are behavioral, and altering your behavior is never ever easy. Some Rules will appear stunningly simple; however, for every Rule, you have to ask yourself: "I may already understand this, but do I do it?" The determination to put in the time and do something, make things occur, is important.

You have Got to Know your status Before You Start

Before we can move forward, we need to understand where we are now. When Robinson Crusoe swam ashore from the shipwrecked boat, the first thing he did was take a look at what guns and stores and ammunition he had. He might assess the circumstance and move forward when he understood that.

So you are going to swim ashore and begin your brand-new life. The very first thing you have to do is to take stock. Discover what you've currently got, what can be used, what can be discarded or discounted, what you owe, what you are owed, what essentially is your net worth.

Try to do a full financial audit on you and your life. If you don't understand where you are prior to you start, you can't truly work efficiently towards ending up being wealthy. It's a wise man who lays out his tools before he begins the task.

This might not be ideal for your situations but I'm sure you understand. Don't be tempted to skip this workout. Even if your monetary scenario is none too rosy, it's excellent to confront truth so that you can take positive action to deal with the situation.

You need to Have a Plan

Why are unwise people and their money so quickly parted? Reason is because the fool doesn't have a plan. If you do not have a strategy, you'll be lured to fritter your money away, spend it instead of investing, or forget the new service concept or career move. If you have a strategy, you know precisely what does and what does not suit it.

The last rule assisted you in the exercise where you are now, and you currently know where you're going (your objective).

The plan provides you with the crucial bit, how you are going to get there. You see, even the best plans need to be modified.

First things first, If you have a task you like and more than happy, then you'll most likely desire to persevere it. If it does not make you sufficient cash, you require a plan to generate earnings in another method. If your task is making you unpleasant and what's worse, keeping you in a poverty trap, then you must prioritize leaving it in your strategy.

Your plan should include capturing the financial control of your life. If you have debts, it will definitely include taking on these as a top priority, ditto costs excesses. The plan might include a career change, investigating a company idea, investing money, or generating some capital so that you can enter the buy-to-lease market. It may well include offering things. A lot of money is created through selling things, whether it's an item, a service, or your time and skill. One of the fundamental truths about getting abundant is that wealth, real wealth comes from doing offers, not from making fees, salaries, or salaries.

An excellent plan today is better than an ideal plan tomorrow. Whatever the plan consists of, just make sure you have one, which you adhere to it. Don't fret; the rest of this book will provide you lots of concepts regarding what your plan might contain. Just keep in mind: Never kick back and wait for somebody to give you money ever.

Get Your Finances Under Control

You may well have enough cash, but it leaks away before you get to spend it. In a whole range of ways taxation, paying interest, lack of usage (not invested effectively), too much invested in the wrong things. Before you can manage your finances, you have to stop the leakages.

If you brought out the exercise in above, you'd have a record of your credit card balances. Greater than you cared to admit? Most likely. We are all motivated to invest in plastic. We are all seduced into acquiring financial obligations regularly monthly. If you want to stop the leakages, cut up all the cards and pay them off.

See and do a fast computation of what levels of interest you are paying. It is exactly your mortgage. Ensure you're not paying more than you have to neglect. If your fixed-rate offer has actually concerned an end, it might be time to examine out the very best deals that are now available.

Keep a record of whatever you spend, everything. Do this for a brief while, even for a week and see where the leaks are. First, you have to know where the money goes, if you are going to be wealthy.

Speculate to Accumulate

All of us know the actor, who achieves overnight popularity after one starring role and everybody states how lucky they should have been. Luck? They starred in every school production. They studied at drama school for 3 years. Worked socks off in some awful soap,

Well, the reality is that you have to speculate to accumulate. You need to be in it to win it. You don't get if you don't wager. No.

I am not suggesting gaming in no opinion having invested in the stock market and having taking recommendations and studying the business and their efficiency, and this is the safest way to gamble, assuming you are staking all on red, which is the highest form of risk in gambling. This is not betting if you work your socks off for 20 years, and lastly, it pays off.

Speculates has, in reality, four meanings-- to go over, to think deeply, to invest, and to believe in something not entirely certain. I believe that summarize our path to success.

- **Discuss:** Talk to all and sundry about wealth and see what others believe and do. Study them closely.
- **Think deeply**: Understand your subject.
- **Invest**: Speculate with your time and effort and life.
- **Believe in something not completely certain**: There are no guarantees; however, you should have the ability to reduce the

chances substantially if you follow the guidelines others have forged for you.

I know you may have believed I suggest you speculate with your hard-earned cash. I don't mean, you to speculate with your time and effort, preparation and planning, energy, and dedication. What you put in is what you'll get out.

Choose Your Attitude to Risk.

Am I going to recommend that money can just be tough won by perilous investments and chancy ventures? No, I'm not. In that case, am I recommending caution which you should carefully hold on to every cent? No, I'm not advocating that either.

What I am suggesting is that it's completely up to you what level of risk you can cope with, it's no good for me to tell you what your risk level must be. You have to decide your attitude and capacity for risk. Personally, I enjoy the idea of sailing close to the wind financially. My mindset is definitely verging on the cautious side, so I don't take the threat. I find the risky schemes where you could blow it all or make a fortune hold some appeal, but I don't indulge in it. When you have young kids for instance with affect your level of risk as the kids comes first, it makes your planning easier. It allows you to tailor how you plan to end up being thriving. Hare or tortoise, I think.

Undoubtedly your mindset will differ depending upon the task.

Things to think about are :

Your age: We cope much better with risk the more youthful we are.

Household dedications: If like me, you have kids, it does make you more cautious. You might be prepared to press it a bit further if they've all left home.

Earnings and/or properties: You need to exercise the portion of your wealth you are prepared to risk. The more you've got, the smaller the danger may be unless you are prepared to risk it all, of course, If you are going to take dangers, then do try to offset them.

Get insurance if you like: - Don't put all your eggs in one basket (more about this later). Consider just how much tension and enjoyment you can deal with.

Look at the timing: long term versus quick returns. Consider how much you can manage to run the risk of worst-case circumstance things.

How much information have you? Insufficient increases in danger. The other thing to contemplate is how you react to the threats of life. Life in itself is risky, and nothing in particular.

How do you cope when things fail? Are you favorable, vibrant, passionate, and up? Or do you get all dismal and depressed and feel like the glass is half empty? Know yourself, and know-how you cope and how you react to changes. And bear in mind that danger doesn't indicate bad. It suggests you don't know how it will all end up.

What is wealth to you? This is one you must sit and meditate on in advance if you are going to get rich. My observation is that rich people usually have actually worked this one out. They understand precisely what, to them, wealth suggests. I have a rich and exceptionally generous good friend who says that he knew long earlier when he was beginning in service that he would consider he had made enough when he wasn't living off the cash he had actually accumulated (which we will call capital). Nor would he be living from the interest on his capital. No, he would consider himself rich when he was living on the interest on the interest on his capital. Sounds good to me.

Now, this good friend understands just how much his interest on the interest is making him, practically by the hour. Therefore if we all go out for a meal in the evening, he knows (a) how much the meal has a cost and (b) how much he has made while consuming a meal, He says that as long as is more than, then he is happy.

This is setting the meaning of wealth quite high, you might think. Maybe you would not wish to set it this high, which's fine naturally. Again, maybe you 'd want to put some kind of figure on it. In the old days, everybody wanted to be a millionaire. Today, there were a lot of people that have houses worth more than that, and they would not consider themselves rich at all and yet have not rather got around to up the ante to wanting themselves, billionaires. *.

Sorry, but to me, a billion might be a million, and I won't be convinced otherwise.

For some individuals, not fretting might mean having enough to spend on any emergency situation that might emerge in your household or home. So how will you specify it? By the variety of cars and trucks you own? Servants? Money in the bank? Value of your house? Portfolio of financial investments?

There are, obviously, no right or wrong answers; however, I do feel that until you've worked this one out, you should not read on. We may aim at anything if we have no target. if we do not have a destination,we can't leave home, or we'll be driving around in circles for hours. If we do not have a meaning, how can we judge or monitor success? If we do not do this, how will you understand if this book has been useful to you? Wealth creation is based on the mindset.

It's Never Too Late to BEGIN Getting Wealthy

Look at Rule 1 again anybody can generate income. And it's not restricted by your age or any other time element. All it needs is that you shift your focus to prospering, and already, things will happen without you needing to do anything more. Undoubtedly if you desire more than the standard that deep space is going to offer you, you will need to do more. By

21

moving your focus, you will set the wheels in motion and success will come to you. And no, this isn't mumbo jumbo. It's a universal fact. No matter how long you have been threading a specific path, poverty, absence of success, whatever, it does not require much of a shift to change course. And modifying course can occur no matter the length of time you've left it. There is no such thing as far too late; It's like being an ocean liner.

CHAPTER FOUR

5 Simple Ways to tap Your Mind Into Attracting Wealth

Knowing how to utilize mind power, and finding out particularly how to use mind power to bring in wealth and abundance, has in fact, been a major focus for most of my life. Along with the technique, I've discovered that making use of mind power works most effectively when it is finished with ease and grace. You do not need to have a tough time to get what you desire in life. Whenever you make a struggle, you push away that which you most desire.

Making use of mind power to alter your life is more like a magic technique than anything else. You merely deceive your mind into thinking that you have what you want, and after that, your life amazingly changes to reveal your new belief. And just like a magic technique, it seems impossible till you learn the strategy, and after that, you understand it is actually really basic.

Yes, I said, very fundamentally. The 5 actions which follow are developed for the complete novice. You can begin today, today, to draw in more prosperity in your life. Here are 5 methods to start quickly.

1. Show Gratitude For Any Money Which Enters Your Life

In order to attract cash into your life, you ought to reveal thankfulness for the cash which is currently in your life. Instead of complaining about how little the cash you have, enjoy gratitude at the many techniques in which you are currently abundant. , if you make more than $25,400 a year, you are in the top 10 percent of wealthy people on this planet. And if you make over $2,182 annually, you have more wealth than 85 percent of the individuals in the world. When you focus on what you have than what you desire, you acknowledge that you ARE currently abundant. Appreciate often for all the riches in your life.

How to utilize this concept today:

The next time cash enters your life, from any source whatsoever, rather of barely finding what has actually happened and psychologically beginning to invest it, utilize a number of moments of time to give thanks to the universe for bringing this money into your life. Whenever you receive an earnings, whenever someone uses your cash for any aspect, each time you discover money, or get a bargain, or save cash in some method, appreciate the truth and stop that money is streaming into your life. Doing this each time cash pertains to you will attract a lot of cash into your life.

2. If You Are Rich, Act As One

This is the basic truth of all mind power work that you need to act as if what you desire is yours already. Therefore act as if you already have the wealth you desire to have. Ask yourself, if I was already abundant, what would I do, how would I act, how would I feel, and after that do, act, and feel in those ways. Of course, you do not require to quit your job and relocate to the South Pacific like you would if you unexpectedly won the lottery, but you begin small, and with each success, you build your method to higher and greater wealth. Consume a little bit better, gown a bit better, go on slightly higher-end vacations, take a cab instead of the bus from time to time, take that course you think you can't pay for or do anything at all that you want to do but think you can not because there is no money. And when performing all these things, bask in happiness at your inner state of wealth, and know that this state will be reflected in your outer world. You'll be astonished at how life offers the important things which bring you happiness.

How to use this principle today:

The next time you will buy something, anything at all, acquire a product that is of a little higher quality and cost than you would usually buy. Even if something just costs a couple of dollars more than what is normal for you to invest, purchase that product and thank deep space for offering your new broadening way of life. Despite the fact that it is a small action, you are beginning to teach your mind that you are expanding your constraints, and as you practice this you will begin to buy more of the important things you desire in your life, and the money will pertain to you to pay for them.

3. Find A Penny, Pick It Up

In order to bring in wealth into your life, your subconscious mind must be open to the concept of wealth flowing to you. You need to be open and responsive to money concerning you from any source whatsoever. This consists of the pennies laying on the street. If you pass a penny on the walkway, and your normal response is simply to overlook it due to the fact that stoop-ing down to get a penny is unworthy the effort, you are telling your subconscious mind that you are not ready to put out effort for money. The amount of money makes no distinction whatsoever. The subconscious mind does not compare one penny and one million dollars. All it knows is how you feel. Naturally, this manifests in lots of other ways also. Whenever you do decline a gift happily, whenever you do not charge somebody for work that you have done for them, or charge them way less than you need to because you feel guilty, and whenever you sell an item for less than it deserves due to the fact that you do not wish to charge excessive, you are creating the same feelings. To begin to be open up to money, in whatever type, and start to accept it flows into your life, even if it's just a cent on the street. How to use this concept today: Simply opt for a walk today and search for cash.

You make sure to discover a minimum of a penny somewhere. Choose it up and thank the universe for the gift of bringing money into your life. Let your subconscious mind know that you are willing and open to accept money from any source. Apply this principle in your working life. If you have actually been undercharging for your services, raise your costs. Ask for a raise if you are not earning what you feel you should. And whenever anyone gives you anything, particularly cash, accept it graciously and appreciate it.

4. Be Open To Money-Making Opportunities.

Major thing that all self-made millionaires concur on is that there are chances every-where if we are just open up to seeing them. You can prove this for yourself by taking a look at your own life. There are most likely lots of times in your past which you reflect to and question what may have happened if you had actually taken a chance at just the correct time. Whether it's apparent things like career changes you let slip by, financial investment chances you didn't think in, or less apparent opportunities like an idea you when had that is now making somebody else abundant, or an industry you might have joined prior to it became saturated if you are like many people when you think about your past opportunities.

The difference between poor and rich individuals is that rich people realize that brand-new chances are always all around us, all the time. You simply require to keep a watch out for the chances, open and keep mind, and be prepared to take advantage when the opportunity shows up. When opportunity meets preparation, I'm sure you've heard the old saying that luck happens. Well, it could not be truer. If you expect to find money-making changes in your life, and you prepare to make the most of them when they come, you will be blessed with more amazing luck than you have ever experienced. How to use this concept today: Get a little notebook and document all the money-making ideas you can think about. It does not matter how foolish or outrageous the concept may appear, however, compose it down anyhow. This does 2 things.

You understand that there are plenty of profitable opportunities around you right now, as there always have been and always will be. This workout will stimulate you to mind to see lucrative opportunities where it might have overlooked them in the past and will assist you to practice to see changes in the future. If you keep including ideas to your notebook consistently, one day, you will see an extreme chance on your list, which is perfect for you. Go for it!

5. Do Something That Makes You Feel Good

This has actually got to be the most convenient profitable recommendations I could ever offer. Do something that makes you feel excellent. When you feel good, your energy arises, and when your energy rises, it draws in more of the things into your life, which makes you feel good.s

28

Could life be any simpler? Not actually, but we are so captured up in the backward thinking about every-one around us that we miss out on the obvious flow of energy. All you really require to bring in more of the good ideas in your life, including more money, is to produce positive energy into the world. The states of happiness and delight literally reorganize the atoms of your world to bring you more joy and joy. Obviously, the reverse is real also. So avoid fear, anger, depression, and invest your time feeling excellent about yourself and your life. Just practice if this is challenging for you. Begin with some little thing which brings you happiness. It could be as simple as viewing a sunset, leasing your favorite movies of all time or taking someone you love out for a dessert or something else. The secret to putting all your effort into those things whole-heartedly, with all your attention, concentrated on the joy vibrating.

This basic act will bring you abundant benefits. How to utilize this principle today: Don't just read this article and think, that sounds excellent, and then go back to your life. Pick something you like to do that brings you joy,probably engage in it today regardless of how big or small it may seem in truth; you do not need to do anything.

All that is necessary is feeling the positive feelings of joy and joy emanating from your soul. One simple way to produce positive emotion is to feel thankfulness for something in your life. Just choose something in your life for which you are really grateful, and vibrate your thankfulness towards it.

If You Start Now, It's Never Too Late

That should get you started. 5 extremely simple actions you can take to begin to broaden the success you experience in your life. However, do not stop there. Never ever let fear or doubt enter your mind. There is absolutely nothing you need to be successful except for the power of your own mind. If you stress that you are not clever enough, not connected enough, not gifted enough, not young enough, or not old enough, you are simply developing limiting beliefs that will manifest in the outdoors world.

All you really require to understand is that the outdoors world is a reflection of the state of your inner mind. Know that you can make every day from this day forward a little bit more joyful and a little bit more abundant and you see your life start to change. It's a moderate and easy treatment, just like letting a plant grow. One day you will suddenly understand that all of your fantastic ideas have ended up being the stunning fruits of beauty and successful life. This short post will point you in the perfect instructions

CHAPTER FIVE

I'm Thinking But I'm Not Growing Rich!

Have you taken a look at "Grow and think Rich," and you have got an intellectual knowledge that you "are what you think about". You have a whole of affirmations about wealth, and you recite them every day. However, you still have no money. Wealth does not appear to be anywhere around.

What's the offer here? According to Napoleon Hill, you have to be filthy stinkin' rich, right? Well, here's the genuine deal: If you're not "Wealth Conscious," then all this thinking and all this validating isn't going to bring you wealth. Thinking and verifying are simply actions you're taking. Nevertheless, they are just part of the series of producing wealth. You merely can't get anywhere if you avoid the first action.

What's the really first action?

To attract wealth, you at first require to BE wealthy. Then, you think rich ideas, speak rich affirmations, and take wealthy action.

"But how can I be rich if I'm not wealthy?" you ask. The rational question, but it's based upon the incorrect presumption that you do not have wealth. You have wealth. You're simply not knowledgeable about it. You have actually constructed a physical reality that prevents you from experiencing Wealth. This can all be discussed with the science of Quantum Physics.

So let's look at some incredibly basic concepts of Quantum Physics that will explain what I'm talking about.

Initially, you most likely understand (a minimum of on an intellectual level) that at a subatomic level, we, and whatever else in the Earth, is Energy. When you have a breakdown of everything, we're all made from the same things, and we're all linked. Deep space is just this huge ocean of energy, vibrating at various frequencies, which offers the illusion of individuation. That is, we experience the impression of separateness from each other, physical things, and wealth because our" senses "are translating the Energy around us in such a method as to create our physical truth. This all occurs in our ideas. So, to simplify things quickly here for the sake of time(another impression), "things" just exist since we observe them. It remains in our observing that things originate. Without our observing, things are just "waves" or possibilities of existence. Physicists agree on this. Our beliefs are an extremely powerful Energy system in our lives. Our beliefs permit or disallow particular experiences in our lives, consisting of wealth. They comprise who we are. We "BE" on the planet according to our beliefs. If we are "being somebody" who is attempting to get wealthy by duplicating affirmations, then that

32

is what our reality will be. We will simply be trying to get wealthy. We have to decide that we are wealthy, contrary to any external physical proof.

That evidence is an impression based upon the belief systems that have directed who we have depended on that point. Because they have money, a really wealthy person isn't wealthy. They have cash, due to the fact that they are rich! That's the distinction that a lot of people have backward! Here's an example to highlight what I indicate: Tony Robbins ended up being a millionaire at a very young age. Due to a series of bad judgments, he lost it. However, within a year, he had it back. How did he do this? HE never lost his wealth. He just lost his money, which is simply a symbol of wealth! Since he is "Wealth Conscious", he actually "magnetically attracts" wealth into his life. He genuinely can't assist it!. It's who he is! And there are thousands out there like him, who attract wealth simply due to the fact that it's who they are. You can make the same choice and have the very same results. Alternatively, a person who had grown up with a "lack of consciousness" can win millions in the lotto and lose it within a year. Their awareness and energy merely can't preserve the destination to Wealth because they aren't "wealthy" in who they are being. Once again, Wealth is a choice. If you aren't currently experiencing wealth, you initially require to realize that abundance is everywhere in truth, it's all there is. Hardship and absence are impressions. You can move your awareness to

Wealth -BE Wealth- by merely making a choice, then your ideas, speech, and action will permit you to experience the wealth that is yours!. This is indeed a complex subject that challenges our core belief systems. However, it is those very belief systems that keep a person in a state of lack. Look at your monetary scenario today, and Look at your core beliefs about Wealth and You, and see if your life isn't a perfect reflection of your beliefs. Then, look where those beliefs might have emanated. When you can as well awaken to yourself that your beliefs produce your truth, instead of the other way around, you have the alternative to genuinely be complimentary to experience a truth of success that you deserve!

CHAPTER SIX

Earn From Facebook

This chapter is everything about how to make cash from the Facebook groups you handle.

We understand it isn't easy, and moderating takes a lot of effort and probably gets you a lot of upset messages. Being one of the administrators of a large Facebook group is tough and stressful. I'm sure you already understand, replying hundreds of messages daily can be very stressful.

Did you understand there are tools you can use to make your adminning procedure simpler, more efficient, and faster to generate income from?

Step 1: Get Group Funnels.

Are you using your Facebook group to produce an email list that you can market to on a continuous basis? No? If your answer is "No" then something must be done to that ASAP.

You need to be speaking to your group members beyond your Facebook group, for a range of factors. Facebook's algorithm can change at any point, this occurred to Facebook pages, and all of a sudden the overall reach went to essentially nothing.

Secondly, your group might get "Zucced" at any point. The account can be shut down easily even without informing you, if you make a post that makes your members mad, and they report you. And all that effort you put into constructing your community? Might just go in vain.

Moving your members over to ending up being email subscribers is how you can mitigate these possible dangers. And think what? Group Funnels does this instantly. As individuals request to join your group and provide their e-mail address in the "address these concerns" area, Group Funnels will add them to your e-mail list, and after that, send them a welcome email right away.

This is a HUGE element of monetizing your list. You can't just develop the email list, you've got to communicate with them upon joining. Group Funnels makes this automated and easy, and it's GDPR certified.

Group funnels will likewise auto-approve potential members based upon the criteria you set. Want possible members to address your subscription approval questions? Group Funnels will car deny them if they do not. Desire to produce a femme-only space, like Sisters in SEO? Group Funnels enables that performance also.

Essentially, Group Funnels can conserve you numerous hours each year on the screening, approval, and lead catching procedures.

It'll do everything, however, make you breakfast in the early morning, and if you admin a large Facebook group, it's an absolute must-have. Plus, you pay when and get lifetime access (so there are no repeating month-to-month fees, it's a one-and-done thing that works for all the groups you manage).

Monetization is pretty easy and automated when you've signed up for this. Even if you do not join Group Funnels, you can still make money off of your members, even if you're a total beginner at this kind of thing.

When you are thinking of monetizing a group can face some obstacle, especially if you don't have a lot of experience. It might feel like it's excessive to even begin.

It's not. You can select any course online and make money from Facebook groups in a very short time period with both marketing and affiliate partners:

Now how can you make money as an Admin? What makes Facebook group interesting to Brands Owners?

There are lot of millions of various groups on Facebook, and some are simpler to generate income from than others. It basically boils down to your specific niche and targeting, with a side of, "how huge is your group?"

Potential marketing and sponsorship partners are going to desire to see an engaged group of people who closely or better yet, similar to there targeted Audiences. This is why targeting the right audiences is a very crucial point; every sponsorship partners will want to consider in other to focus on their product or services sales .

What possible advertising and sponsorship partners don't desire to wish to see is a great deal of noise or spam in the group. This signals to the marketing supervisors that the spam and sound are going to drown out their message, that makes your Facebook group appear like a less appealing place for advertisement and marketing dollars.

Likewise, bad, spammy posting devalues your group in general if you are considering to make money from your group, it's really crucial that you manage and monitor what's published in your group.

Ensure the Group Content is of High Quality & On Target.

Think about upgrading your modding requirements if you're not currently ruling your Facebook group throne with an iron fist. Being the admin of a group, you have to focused on providing value to your group members. This implies keeping posts restricted to those that provide worth or are of actual interest to members.

Potential brand partners are also going to wish to see a lot of engagement on the posts. The number of posts daily exist? The number of comments and likes? Spammers in your Facebook group post crap links.

It's not likely that the brand name's message will be heard if the number of posts per day is too high. This can be worked around, with plans that consist of multiple posts (and announcements!), as well as the promise to pin a post for a set quantity of time.

Think it or not; it's even possible to generate income by tagging other groups. Imagine tagging a group with 750, 000 members, the audience must be extremely targeted and, for that reason, the types of the brand you are promoting will varies.

If all your group members have similar characteristics, then you can monetize the group, by claiming opportunities to promote brands for people. Groups around expert interests and skill sharing, hobbies, travel, adorable images of pets (I'm sure there's a pet dog toy company thinking about that target audience) practically any big Facebook group can be generated income from, as long as the target group is clear.

How big does your Facebook group requirement to be to generate income?

The brief answer is, it depends upon your group's niche. The minimum Facebook group size that would draw in a brand partner for sponsorship is probably in the area of 10,000 members or more, however, if your audience is extremely targeted and the dollar worth of the widgets you're selling to them is high enough, 3,000-5,000 may suffice.

Imagine having group members worth 100,000 or more and the group is extremely targeted (your members all share a similar interest, which can be marketed to), you should have no problem turning your Facebook group into a well-oiled money-making machine.

As the owner of a big Facebook group, here's something that you must know about brand names:

It doesn't matter the number of Facebook likes the brand name page has, the battle to reach those individuals who liked the page all those years back is genuine.

Thanks to Facebook's algorithm updates, brand names simply do not get the page reach they used to. This suggests that if brand names want their posts to reveal up in the news feeds of individuals who like their page, they require to spend for it.

Aside from retargeting traffic by means of Facebook pixels, Facebook's advertisement targeting is less than excellent and requires a lot of A/B screening to get. This A/B screening is pricey, and marketing firms are often shooting darts in the dark at target audiences till you strike on something with a lower cost per click than the others.

Some brand names are starting to enter the Facebook group game, but it can be a long road to development (as you might know!) and rather honestly, a lot of professional social media marketers do not have the savvy, budget or time to successfully grow groups for their customers.

This is the reason why a large Facebook group, which is currently well-targeted and has lots of members, additional attractive to online marketers .

Another essential note: there is presently no chance for brand names to straight target members of specific Facebook groups with ads.

This implies that if a brand wishes to promote on a particular Facebook group, it needs to strike an offer with the admin of the group, definitely, you will be getting some cool cash!

Most brands will be ready to pay you any dime to get on the front page of a group with over thousands of members that are extremely targeted audiences that heavily overlap with their own.

This can get complex, and this area could probably be 5-10 different posts, we'll try to get to producing those private guides soon. In the meantime, here's a top-level summary of what you must be performing in order to monetize your Facebook group(s) to the max level possible.

As an admin, you can easily sell some sponsored posts for affiliate partners, but you should not restrict yourself to those two options when it concerns making money from Facebook groups. You should treat your group as the service that it is if you're going to monetize your Facebook page and accept ad money from brand names.

This business can offer at anytime time. Depending upon your group's membership, it's completely possible that a brand name will offer to buy your Facebook group (currently, it looks like that doesn't violate their TOS). You need to begin making it as attractive as possible to possible purchasers now if that's the goal.

Here's what you can also be doing if you're looking to make money with your Facebook groups long-term:

1. Build a website rich with material that delivers value.

Tag groups aside, almost every large Facebook group should likewise have a similarly-branded site with content establishing who your target audience is and the value your brand name delivers to them.

You ought to have an "About" page describing your group and its mission/target audience, plus a media page where you note any press coverage you've received (more on how to get that media protection below). Ask group members to compose guest posts associated with your target market, build-out that material yourself, etc

Be sure to establish Facebook tracking pixels on your site, so you can remarket to the individuals who have been on your website (this can assist you to grow the group even quicker, and offer more value to brand partners considering that you'll likewise have the ability to use remarketing services).

Develop a series of downloadable possessions.

This will help you develop a big list of e-mail customers you can continue to reach out to overtime. Email marketing can have a huge effect on your ability to deliver sales for brand partners (and make more money for yourself in the procedure).

You desire to establish a large e-mail list because it's going to draw in more brand name partners-- and you'll make money substantially more as an outcome of your increased reach. Build your email list by producing downloadable properties that people really desire (belief guides, lists, lists of resources, etc.),

Learn SEO, create material and create organic traffic.

You'll likewise acquire more Facebook group members. Think about your Facebook group as a material marketing maker, that's how your marketing and affiliate partners are looking at it, so you may as well take advantage of it on your own too.

Here's why SEO is so crucial: if you do it right, it'll develop into a huge passive income stream particularly when it concerns affiliate marketing business.

If you do not have a site or have one with low traffic, it will not necessarily derail a Facebook marketing offer if your group has a lot of engaged members. If you're looking to make the most cash from Facebook groups that you manage, you ought to build out a bigger platform than Facebook.

SEO will help reveal that you do not just have a large Facebook group worth marketing to, but likewise, extremely targeted website traffic brand partners can also get value from. And it'll drive affiliate sales, plus present more individuals to your Facebook group.

5. Create a press set.

What should your Facebook group press kit consist of?

- Your Facebook group stats
- Demographic/basic information about the members of your group
- Site traffic statistics
- Email details
- A rate card outlining the sponsorship and ad plans you provide
- Case research studies from past collaborations
- Producing this press kit is last in this list, however not least, you'll be able to close a lot more sponsorship and advertising offers if you have a sleek looking press kit.
- You also require to create a list of prices and bundles. Generally, brand names are searching for a continuous relationship if the partnership works, and we 'd advise the minimum bundle be for three posts expanded over a week or so.
- Develop some plan choices for sponsored posts, and put a cost on it based upon your group size/reach/influence. Make it clear that you're open to concepts from the brand partners, too.

As you create case studies showing your sponsored deals/affiliate promos work well, upgrade your press set to consist of all these details.

Construct your e-mail list.

As described earlier on, in this chapter, you need to NOT depend on Facebook to be a good-hearted source of revenue forever. Anything can alter at any point, which is why you should move your members to other spaces where you can market to them.

Like, for instance, e-mail. Email marketing has an average ROI of 37:1. That's higher than social networks marketing and simply about any other digital marketing strategy.

This means you need to be building your email list and e-mail marketing system, advertisers are going to want in on it! You can likewise use affiliate collaborations to monetize your e-mail list, which will pull double duty on the income-generating front.

CHAPTER SEVEN

Earn from Twitter

You are wondering how to make cash on Twitter? Whether you're a business or a blogger owner, you likely have a Twitter account to promote your brand or company.

Because Twitter is one of the greatest social network platforms with 126 million daily active users, there is a load of people you can introduce to your business. You tweet continuously and hope that simply some of those 126 million individuals see your tweets and inspect you out.

In this chapter, we'll let you in on some incredible methods to generate income on Twitter. But before we reveal to you how to earn money on Twitter, you need to develop your Twitter profile and your following initially.

Twitter is a great marketing tool, and it can be used in a variety of various methods to generate income. Some of them are direct, while others make it through a funnel leading to your site. How do you use Twitter to generate income? One of these concepts may apply.

Automated Spam

Here's one thing you can do, though I don't advise it. Systems like this one deal to set you up with a system that lets you "create automated earnings" and do extremely little to hide the reality that all they're doing is spamming Twitter. You install this app and your account is taken control of by the spammer, who is offering retweets or discusses or some other form of engagement on a website like Fiverr. When someone goes to purchase engagement, the spammer presses a button, and your account-- and a thousand others-- all carry out the action he wants.

Utilize a Monetized Shortlink

There are different services that you can earn from by creating short links. An example is **bit.ly.** They come up with material that individuals desire to see, and clickbait is very good since you are engaging in ad view revenue, one needs as many clicks and views. You're shooting for the least expensive typical denominator for content here, the kind of things that reveals up as related when people go to Buzzfeed. Take the link and shorten it with a monetized shortener like **Adf.ly** and publish it.

Adfly Earnings

When individuals discover your tweet, either because they follow you or since of the hashtags or search terms you use, they'll want to click the link. When they click the link, they see your advertisements and might click them. This gets you paid. The more individuals who do this, the more you earn.

The disadvantage of this method is the quantity of money it makes. That is to state, how little it makes. It's okay if all you want is weekly beer cash, but you aren't going to grow into a living wage out of this.

The obstruction to this method today is discovering a generated income from a URL shortener that works on Twitter. Ad.Fly is understood to be limited or obstructed entirely on Twitter, as are some other shorteners that Twitter has flagged as malicious. Finding the ideal shortener to make you some money is half the work of this technique, which's not since the other half is very little.

Utilize a Twitter Peddler Service

There used to be a service called TweetPeddler that permitted any Twitter user to sign up and begin making profits by posting sponsored tweets as spent for by other TweetPeddler users. The idea was that you would say, "hey, I have X follows, and I tend to publish about Y subjects." The advertiser would decide you're worth $3 for a tweet and would pay that much for you to publish a message they develop. This was automated using an app, so you didn't need to deal with the advertisers straight. This particular service enabled you to set the price of your tweets, so you might filter out the most affordable priced marketers and ensure the ones who wish to use you are willing to pay.

Sponsored Tweet ExampleTweetPeddler is gone nowadays. Twitter chose it was abusive, and not a good factor; it was utilized often to spam the lower-priced users with hateful or racist tweets. Sure, those users made a little cash before they were prohibited, but Twitter discovered it better just to close down the app completely. That doesn't mean, nevertheless, that there aren't other comparable services out there.

All of these services allow you to set your rate, or will evaluate your following and your reputation in order to pick the niche and the worth of your tweets. They're all variations on the very same thing, paying you to make tweets as advertisements for the advertisers in concern. It's up to you to decide where your line is drawn, how often you're prepared to post ads, and how much you desire to try to make from the platform.

Grow an Account and Sell Advertising.

This approach is pretty much the same as the previous one, except you're not using a service to do it. When you take the time to filter your potential marketers thoroughly, you have a better possibility of making sure the individuals who promote on your feed are going to fit in.

Essentially, you wish to try to find the sort of people you would currently recommend. A player might search for gaming-related affiliate programs through stores like GMG, or they might search for a review website that would spend for a bit more exposure. They do not desire to be a shill for the next "shovelware title", so they filter who they're willing to market for.

Preferably, this will get you a more significant per-tweet earnings, but you'll need to put a lot more work into it. It's not almost as automatic as the previous technique. That stated, if you're persistent and can get a decent set of advertisers, you'll be able to make a fair bit of money.

Some websites help facilitate that too. The huge one is MyLikes, which works for other social feeds also. It's similar to the more automatic websites above, but gives you a lot more control, both over individuals who promote with you and the costs you charge.

Promote Affiliate Products to Followers:

Another method to monetize your Twitter account is by promoting affiliate items. When most people think about affiliate marketing, they think of blog writers promoting affiliate items on their sites. However, you can promote affiliate products on Twitter to generate income too. Affiliate marketing is merely the procedure for promoting other individuals' items. You make a commission when someone buys that item through the link you shared.

Among the fantastic features of affiliate marketing is that you can get going as a newbie, you do not require to have a

50

substantial Twitter following to be accepted into affiliate marketing programs. To discover affiliate items, you can promote on Twitter, develop an account on an affiliate marketing network like:

- ShareASale
- Amazon Associates
- FlexOffers
- ClickBank

Don't promote any affiliate item you stumble upon, however. If you promote a heap of different products without any rhyme or factor, your Twitter profile will not be focused, and your target market won't understand what they're getting from each day to the next.

Simply take a look at all of the different types of affiliate items you can find on ClickBank.

To be successful in affiliate marketing, it's sensible to choose a niche. Choose a niche that you're knowledgeable about which you're passionate about too. A food blogger should stick with food, cooking, and white wine products because they know that their audience is interested in those types of products. Plus, their audience will trust their recommendations in the classification and be more likely to purchase.

Do not spam your followers with affiliate links, either. Mix them in with your regular material so that you don't annoy your followers. Too numerous suspicious links can get your account suspended too.

Quick Tip: Want to set up your affiliate program? Take a look at our guide!

At some time, you may begin to realize that the worth of a tweet is not always in the tweet itself, but in the message. It's tough to make a great deal of money selling specific tweets because they have a repaired and typically low value. You have to tweet a lot, which drives away your users, which drops your following and your track record, which devalues your tweets even more.

Instead, why not make some money "selling" the essential things you currently like to discuss? That's what affiliate marketing is everything about, though many online marketers go the other route and find items to sell and then pretend it's what they enjoy to talk about. Either path works, so long as you develop a following.

The standard procedure of affiliate marketing on Twitter is quite simple. Initially, you construct a large following, at least a few thousand people. Remember, engagement rates on Twitter are quite bad, and you need more than simply basic engagement to make cash from affiliate marketing.

Ideally, you will develop this audience out of individuals who have an interest in the subject you're covering. These people are interested in you since you speak about that subject, you share a post about that subject, you curate content about that subject, etc. You end up being a center for individuals to see the material in the industry, which's what's essential.

You register for an affiliate program as soon as you have gathered this audience. You can do this through an affiliate network, or through individual recommendation programs. Amazon Affiliates is a fine example of a network that gives you access to millions of items, while something like Massdrop is an example of something that just applies to the one website with a restricted scope.

Now, peppered in throughout your other regular posts, you start promoting products. If you're promoting through Amazon, all you truly need to do is find an industry item and link it utilizing the Amazon Affiliates short link you're given. You can produce these quickly when you're a member of the affiliates program; just navigate to the item page and click the "produce short link" button.

From there, you're done. Any time someone clicks that link and goes on to purchase anything from Amazon, you get a commission from it. It's not a large commission, obviously; Amazon takes the majority of the cash. Given that it can apply to anything on Amazon, it can work out to be rather significant.

There are lots of affiliate networks and millions of deals out there, so there's room for just about anyone. The technique is getting a large adequate and engaged enough audience to really make a good quantity of money about it. Thankfully, there's a lot of details about affiliate marketing out there, and as soon as you get begun with it on Twitter, you can shift it to a site-based company.

Use Twitter to Sell Off-Site Products.

Mentioning having a site-based service, you can have that too. A lot of individuals out there have businesses or blogs that have their own money-making methods. You might be offering items, you could be running affiliate advertisements, you could be monetizing through PPC or PPM ads, or whatever else you wish to do. You might even be hyping up the website to sell it prior to repeating the procedure.

The point is, Twitter can be used as part of a marketing method as well as merely a sales website. Use Twitter to end up being a content hub, like I point out in the affiliate marketing section. They do not really care if you're the one selling them or not, so long as you're honest about it.

The only time you encounter issues with this is when you begin lying and concealing your connection to promote high worth but poor quality deals. Do not attempt to sell it on Twitter; it simply won't work if you would not vouch for a product.

Offer Twitter Growth Consulting Services.

You might reach a point where your marketing is stopping working or your service falters; however you do not wish to get out of the game simply yet. This is another chance, think it or not. What you can do here is rely on the other side of the video game. Don't be the one selling products or growing an audience; be the one to teach others how to do those things.

If you can show that you can grow a Twitter account in the space of a couple of months, you can put that knowledge to work. Start a blog site about growing a Twitter following and offer your services as an expert.

There are a substantial number of people out there looking to enter Twitter, either to promote their own businesses or to offer their products or affiliate deals. Having "been there and done that" you can offer suggestions, offer tools, and typically assist these people to achieve their goals. All of this for a relatively high per-hour cost that individuals want to pay, which makes you more general than you might be making with active marketing.

The finest part is that consulting and marketing are not actually mutually special. You can keep up with an affiliate service or an item sales company while also providing your consulting proficiency and even more to improve your earnings. You just, you know, have to actually have the capability and the experience to make great on your consulting claims. You're not going to go far in the consulting world if you don't actually have the skills to back up your claims.

Use Sponsored Tweets.

Want to make money just for sending out a tweet? You can do that with sponsored tweets.

When you have a strong presence on Twitter with a large following of engaged fans, other businesses will pay you to tweet about their items, services, or brand name. If you're actually popular on Twitter, you can merely reach out to brands you like and share the benefits of promoting their item to your audience with a paid tweet. There are a number of online platforms that will assist you link with business looking to pay for tweets. A number of them are:

SponsoredTweets.

SponsoredTweets is a platform where companies can browse for and get in touch with Twitter influencers.

PaidPerTweet.

PaidPerTweet lets businesses access countless top Twitter users, both standard and celeb users. Prices range from $1 to $10,000, depending on the influencer, use paidpertweet to monetize twitter.

As you can see, if you're an individual with a popular Twitter account, you can make money tweeting. But likewise, the business can purchase sponsored tweets from influencers to promote their business to a whole new audience of people that wish to buy from you.

Promote Your Own Products

If you sell your own products, a fantastic method to make money on Twitter is by promoting them to your followers. Given that your followers are already following you, they're most likely to be thinking about the items you use.

A restricted time sale will have your Twitter fans hurrying to your website to snag that awesome offer prior to it's far too late.

By offering items on Twitter, you can introduce your products to millions of online consumers on Twitter, instead of reaching only your existing website visitors.

According to studies, Twitter users shopped online 6.9 times a month, while non-users went shopping online simply 4.3 times a month. Plus, Twitter users planned to spend 21.7% more than non-users in a 6 month time duration.

Generate Traffic for Your Website

Even if your business doesn't offer products, you can still utilize Twitter to generate traffic for your website or create more leads for a service-based service.

Ali Marten, owner of the popular food blog site Gimme Some Oven, shared this post on Twitter to let her fans understand about the latest recipe on her site.

Sharing your most current post on Twitter will help more users discover your website, improve your website traffic, and grow your blogging career.

You can even be proactive about producing traffic and leads by browsing for pertinent threads and conversations on Twitter.

When it comes to a service-based service like a dental practitioner's workplace, you might search Twitter for keywords like "looking for dental practitioners" or "dentists in [your city]" Begin up a discussion when you discover tweets from people that are looking for dental professionals.

Reply to their tweet by saying something like, "Hey Sarah, I see that you're searching for dental professionals in the location" and leave a link to your company site.

Build an Email List

Building an email list is one of the finest ways to create more sales for your service. With email marketing, you can message your customers straight to share company news or your most current post, announce new items, promote flash sales, and more. According to WPForms, automated e-mails can increase income by as much as 320%.

To build an email list, produce an exit-intent popup using OptinMonster to get the attention of your website visitors prior to they leave your site.

Offering a lead magnet, which is a giveaway like a guide, list, ebook, or design template, in exchange for your visitors' email addresses is a great way to grow your e-mail list quickly.

How do you grow your email list on Twitter?

It's easy! All you need to do is share your lead magnet on Twitter in addition to a link to your e-mail list opt-in landing page Here's how Talia Wolf does it. When they land on her profile, Notice how she likewise pins this tweet so that it's the very first thing users see.

With this method for making money on Twitter, you can turn your Twitter followers into customers and, after that, into consumers with targeted e-mail marketing projects.

6. Offer Customer Service

Offering quality customer service is necessary for any effective organization. While supplying customer care does not necessarily help you generate income directly, it can assist you generate more leads and keep your existing consumers. In truth, according to HelpScout, 7 out of 10 U.S. consumers say they've spent more money to do service with a business that provides fantastic service

And today, customers want quicker and easier customer support than ever in the past. Which is why you need to be using Twitter to supply customer care. Some big companies like UPS have entire Twitter accounts devoted to customer support. You don't need to own a huge company to provide incredible customer support on Twitter.

All you need to be is be available to your consumers and assist them to fix their problems in a quick way-- which will help your company drive more sales. Being there for your clients 24/7 is nearly possible, unless ... you use a **Twitter chatbot.**

A Twitter chatbot can be offered for your consumers day and night and utilizes artificial intelligence (AI) to address client questions. For example, have a look at how Patron Tequila has the ability to make cash with a Twitter bot.

In this case, the chatbot suggests various items the customer ought to purchase for their unique event. It's like the consumer has their very own personal consumption.

Developing a Twitter chatbot appears tough, but don't worry. You can utilize a tool like ManyChat to produce a Twitter bot for your organisation easily.

Run a Giveaway

Running a giveaway appears like an excellent way to promote your company and construct brand name awareness, but does it really help you generate income?

Want evidence? KnivesShipFree.com, an eCommerce shop selling premium knives, utilized a giveaway to turn window-shoppers into clients and created over $10,000 in sales.

So, if you wish to earn money on Twitter, try running a gift You can utilize a tool like RafflePress, which is among the most powerful giveaway plugins on the marketplace, to develop and handle your free gift easily. With RafflePress, you can create a giveaway landing page in no time using their drag and drop giveaway home builder (and there's a FREE version).

Then, promote your giveaway on Twitter as BomiBox did below. They consisted of an attractive image of the giveaway reward, contest details, and #Giveaway. In your post, don't forget to add a link to your RafflePress giveaway landing page so your followers can quickly enter your contest.

Another great feature of RafflePress is their verified bonus offer actions. Benefit actions give users extra entries for completing specific tasks, like going to a page on your website, following you on Twitter, joining your e-mail list, and far more.

So, by running your giveaway with RafflePress, you can create more sales and grow your Twitter following at the very same time.

Create Twitter Ads

Another method to generate more sales for your company is by producing Twitter Ads. Twitter Ads will help your service reach more people online-- not just your current followers, however other users on Twitter too. The more people that know your business, the more sales you can make.

Twitter Ads are so reliable because you're able to show your ad to simply the ideal individuals. You can show your Twitter Advertisement to users based on their specific interests, demographics, and even their activity on Twitter.

By utilizing targeted Twitter Ads, you can promote your organization to lots of users that have an interest in exactly what you're offering.

So, when a user sees your Twitter Ad in their feed and thinks "Wow, that's just what I needed!", they'll be more most likely to click on your Ad and purchase.

Monetize Your Twitter Presence

On YouTube, creators can monetize their channels, which lets them location ads in their videos and live streams. When an ad is viewed or clicked, the creator generates income from those marketers.

A couple of years ago, Twitter rolled out the Twitter Media Studio, which lets material developers monetize their existence on Twitter.

Twitter Media Studio lets you put in-stream video ads and in-stream video sponsorships right into your brand-safe Twitter video content so that you can generate income directly from the platform. Other functions of Twitter Media Studio include:

<u>Producer:</u> Broadcast expert live streams, promote and schedule live streams, and produce immediate highlights of your stream with LiveCut.

<u>Library:</u> Manage all of your videos, images, and GIFs in one location. You can also add user roles and consents across your group.

<u>Analytics:</u> Measure your performance on Twitter by viewing metrics of your tweets and incomes from monetized videos.

Setting Up A Twitter Account

Let's take an appearance at what you can do to develop a terrific Twitter profile and attract your target audience.

Step 1 to Making Money on Twitter: Create A Killer Twitter Profile

Obviously, if you want to earn money on Twitter, you require a Twitter profile. Not simply any Twitter profile. To earn cash from tweeting, your Twitter profile needs to be set up for success.

It must have a branded look with profile photo and Twitter Cover picture, a matching username and manage, a quick description of what OptinMonster is/does, and a link to the site.

Remember, when developing your Twitter profile, be sure to include:

- A profile photo of yourself or your company logo design
- A pertinent username and Twitter deal with (your name or company name).
- An engaging bio.
- If relevant, a link to your website or blog.
- A completed Twitter profile will assist your followers to learn more about you and develop a relying on relationship with you or your brand name.

Speaking of followers, let's discover how to get some in the next step.

Step 2 to Making Money on Twitter: Grow Your Following.

With 0 fans on Twitter, your tweets won't get much engagement, which injures your chances of earning money on Twitter.

So, how do you get followers on Twitter?

Well, the easiest method to get more fans naturally is merely by being active on the platform. Being active on Twitter simply means that you require to post regular content and communicate with other users on Twitter by retweeting, preference, and commenting.

Ensure the content you share on Twitter relates to your niche or your industry and utilize hashtags to broaden your reach.

Being active on Twitter will attract more followers to your profile, and it will assist you in keeping the fans you currently have too.

Some other easy ways to grow your Twitter following are:

- Follow individuals relevant to your industry/target audience.
- Include your Twitter deal with to your email signature.
- Promote your Twitter profile on other social network platforms.
- Embed your Twitter feed to your site.
- You can likewise create a "Follow United States on Twitter" popup on your site to grow your following.

By producing a "Follow Us on Twitter" popup, you can take the website traffic you currently have and turn those users into Twitter fans. Now that you know how to develop an optimized Twitter start earning!

Now you know how to monetize Twitter and drive more sales for your service using among the most popular social media platforms.

So, rather of simply visiting to Twitter and sending a couple of tweets in hopes of drawing in clients, you now have a plan that makes sure to bring in cold, difficult cash.

CHAPTER EIGHT

Earn from Youtube

Over a billion people utilize YouTube. That number sounds big enough by itself, however, to actually it put it into perspective, that's about a third of the individuals on the internet. And some of those users are on YouTube almost every day.

We can quite well bet that if you're reading this, you're one of the more than a billion individuals that view videos on YouTube, so you know that when you view a video, you generally see an ad. Naturally, some of the cash of those advertisements goes to Google. In many cases, though, individuals who produced the video get a cut too.

YouTube has paid $2 billion to content developers and rights holders that have taken the proper actions to declare their part of the revenues.

Who Can Make Money on YouTube?

YouTube does pay content developers. The bad news is that the majority of individuals that fill videos to YouTube will never see a cent. And numerous of those that do actually get paid will not be making enough to leave their day jobs.

For you to earn anything, your videos need to attract not only a lot of viewers but likewise audiences that want to engage with the advertisements. That means they need to in fact watch a decent portion of the ad before clicking that "skip" button (you understand the one, you've most likely clicked great deals of times yourself), or click on the link that shows up at the bottom of the screen during the advertisement.

Those who are popular enough can reach the point of earning thousands on the site, but it's an unusual couple of that reaches that point. The platform hosts billions of videos, so your competitors are pretty strong.

So do not stop your task or base all your future hopes on YouTube. If you like creating videos anyhow and you want to see if your pastime can begin to pay off, it doesn't harmed to take the correct actions that make it possible to get paid by YouTube.

Note: In early 2018, YouTube made changes to its Partner Program. To be eligible for monetization, accounts should have accumulated 4,000 hours of watch time in the past year and reach 1,000 customers. Follow the steps below to opt-in to the program so as soon as you reach that threshold, you can generate income on YouTube!

Steps to YouTube Monetization

Here's what you need to do if you want at least an opportunity to make money on YouTube.

Step 1: Set up your YouTube channel.

If you currently have a Google account, as many people do, then use that to log in to YouTube. If you do not yet have a Google account, start by creating one here, and after that go on and log in to YouTube.

Click the Upload button in the leading right of the screen, and you'll receive a prompt to develop a channel when you're logged in. Click "Create Channel", and you're done.

Step 2: Create your video plan.

Now you require to make some choices about the videos you're going to upload. If you desire to get subscribers and motivate engagement, then your objective should be to build a following of individuals that like your videos enough to sign up for your channel and return once again and again. Make sure you understand the audience you want to reach.

Brainstorm a list of subjects for videos that will appeal to that audience. Develop a schedule for your videos. If you regularly upload at regular intervals, you're more likely to get and bring in fans.

You might desire to spend some time throughout this action, browsing some of the most popular videos in your space to see what people react to. You don't want to do the same thing that other content developers are doing, but you can obtain some insights into what works best to apply to your videos.

Your plan does not have to be set in stone, but having a plan in place to direct you will help guarantee you persevere and approach your YouTube channel in a strategic manner in which's most likely to settle.

Step 3: Enable monetization.

Now click the Account icon in the leading right corner of the screen and then click on the Creator Studio button that appears.

On the menu on the left side of the screen click Channel, then pick Status and Features in the submenu that opens up under it.

Now you'll see the option to make it possible for monetization. (Note: You may have to provide Google with your country before the enable button appears, simply follow the guidelines the screen provides to do so).

Step 4: Sign up for Google AdSense.

When you've made it possible for monetization, clicking the Monetization alternative in the menu will take you to a page where you can start the process of establishing your Google AdSense account, or connecting an account you currently need to your channel.

Just choose "Next" and follow the guidelines to create your account.

Step 5: Start packing (excellent) videos.

Now the fundamental stuff is covered, and you've reached the difficult part. Create the videos you decided on in your plan and begin submitting them to the channel.

We currently advise that your videos need to be quite great and attract a large audience for you to make any money, so invest some actual time working to make sure your videos are specific instructional, amusing, or special so that they'll get attention in a congested space.

Step 6: Promote your videos.

Even if your videos are amazing, people won't instantly know to come trying to find you. Research the finest practices for enhancing your YouTube videos for search so it's much easier for people to discover you that method.

Share your videos on social media. Talk them up to family and friends members that might be interested. Eventually, you'll reach a tipping point where your customers begin to do some of the promotion for you if people enjoy them. In the meantime, you need to put some real effort into getting your videos in front of individuals.

Step 7: Keep an eye on your analytics.

At initially, your analytics won't inform you all that much. As you get increasingly more viewers, however, you'll be able to utilize your YouTube Analytics to determine which kinds of subjects or videos get the finest outcomes, both in terms of views and engagement. You'll likewise be able to find out a bit about who your audience is and how they're finding their method to your videos so you can fine-tune your promotion efforts based upon what's working.

Use the information to continuously enhance your video plan. The better your videos perform, the more you'll have the ability to make in the long run.

If you do not make much headway with making cash on YouTube, don't be shocked. You will not be wasting your time even if you never ever reach a payday if you have enjoyable developing your videos. Keep your expectations realistic and stick to making videos of a type that you understand you'll take pleasure in producing, so the possibility of generating income will simply be a nice bonus if or when you attain it.

CHAPTER NINE

Earn from Instagram

To make cash on Instagram,.you need a big following of individuals. The more followers that you have, the more cash you will make. With that being stated, acquiring followers on Instagram can be gruelling and extremely tiring.

Always keep in mind the endgame, and continuously advise yourself why you are doing this in the very first location. There will be days during your Instagram journey when you just don't feel like publishing, and seem like you are making no development. This is all part of the process. Getting a following on Instagram and developing a network of specific niche related fans is something that requires a ridiculous quantity of perseverance and perseverance.

You do not need always to be smart to earn money on Instagram, in fact, any person can do it. The abilities that you require are only perseverance and determination like I said above. You are more than capable of building accounts that will have over 1 million fans if you have those two qualities.

The Time Frame.

Now that I have actually explained how hard this journey is going to be, you are most likely wondering how long it is going to take before you begin seeing real results on Instagram. Personally, it took me around a year to construct a 200,000 fan Instagram page, and 2 1/2 years to build a 1 million follower Instagram page once you pass the 1 million fan mark, you will easily be making over $100,000 each year, presuming that a large portion of your fans is engaged.

When you have a page with 1 million followers, it will be a lot simpler for you to grow even more pages and expand on to other social media platforms. I will explain all of this later in the book and will teach you how to grow on social media exponentially.

Simply remember that the first milestones are constantly the hardest. The first thousand followers and the very first 100,000 fans will constantly be more difficult than the next.

Picking your Niche.

Now that you have a little bit of background info, and a little bit of motivation, let's get right into starting your service on Instagram.

The initial step is to pick your niche. This can be pets, cats, trucks, travel images, funny memes, fascinating quotes, organization quotes, etc. simply ensure that whatever you pick, you are extremely thinking about the subject. You are going to be working with your niche every single day, so you desire to ensure that it's something that you take pleasure in.

You'll want to head over to Instagram and inspect out how many other pages are in the same specific niche as you. When looking, you desire to make sure that there as at least one other page that has 1 million fans in the same general category of people will not have an interest in it.

An example of a great niche is trucks, and truck associated posts. Trucks, on the other hand, is a specific niche that can be broadened upon and broken down into sub-niches. Let's state that for your first Instagram page, you decide to develop a general trucks fan page. Not a bad idea. From there, when that account begins to grow, you can expand by developing other Instagram pages that focus on Ford trucks, Chevy trucks, and attempt I state its Dodge trucks. The very same concept can be used within an Instagram page about puppies or canines. As soon as your main page begins to pick up traction, you can then broaden by developing smaller sized pages focusing on different types of pet dog types such as pugs, German shepherds, or whatever.

The primary page, or the basic specific niche page, is what will be generating the majority of traffic. The smaller sized sub-niche pages is what you will use to laser target your followers. Consider how much easier it would be to offer a pug T-shirt to a fan page about pugs rather than a basic young puppy fan page.

So just to summarize, select a specific niche that you like and have an interest in, but make certain it's broad enough that you can zoom in, on more targeted niches. After you've come up with that specific niche, compose it down on a notepad. Now do some research study and go. Learn how many other Instagram pages remain in that exact same niche, and see the number of fans they have. The objective is to discover a niche with at least one page over 1 million followers and to find a page that you could exceed with better quality posts.

A great deal of the popular Instagram pages nowadays are run by people who quite frankly don't care about the quality of their posts. They publish blurred photos and do not even trouble to write a caption. Why? Well, since they entered the game early. These types of accounts more than likely started their fan pages right is Instagram was ending up being significantly popular. I've seen many pages with millions of fans that post very bad images. Anyone, especially you, can do a better task. When you find a lousy Instagram page that has over 1 million fans in the specific niche that you're interested in, you must get delighted.

Keeping completion Game in Mind

When choosing your Instagram specific niche, it's essential to have some sort of end video game or objective in mind. How are you preparing to monetize your Instagram page? Are you going to create a web store? Are you going to offer shoutouts? If you're going to offer shoutouts, the number of large business are out there that could possibly be intrigued? Simply have some sort of concept.

The majority of Instagram niches can be generated income from in some method shape or form. It's simply a matter of finding what your Instagram followers truly desire. The only specific niches that are incredibly tough to monetize are celebrity fan pages and pages connected to particular films etc. Many of the time, fan pages gradually disappear, and the followers end up being disinterested with the motion picture once it has been out for a couple of years. The only Instagram page that I've seen able to generate income from in this kind of specific niche was a Harry Potter fan page, and they had a webshop offering replica wands for a steep rate. Now although this may have been a great idea, you'll desire to pick a niche that is long term, something isn't a trend and something that will still be around in ten years.

Choosing Your Username.

Once you've done your research and have a niche in mind (something you're interested in), it's time to choose a username. Usernames require to be basic, unforgettable, and straight to the point. The much better your username, the more of an advantage you will have on Instagram. Here's some standard guidelines:

Do not use numbers in your username.

Using numbers in your username will only puzzle individuals and will injure your ranking on Instagram's search. If you begin a page called "puppyphotos31" that posts puppy memes, what's to stop another person from making a page called: "puppyphotos32." It will simply leave everyone very baffled. The only exception is if the numbers are directly connected to your niche, such as "420humor.". Utilize your specific niche's keyword firstly. Trucksdaily will constantly be more reliable username than dailytruckposts.

When looking for a username, you want to make sure that your primary keyword is initially, as that is what individuals will be looking for. Underscores are okay if you are separating words. I, in fact, own an Instagram page with a highlight that gained followers very quickly. Initially, I was doubtful about utilizing an underscore, but it in fact showed to be more reliable because I might isolate my keyword. Something like "trucks_daily" is a truly great username. When utilizing underscores, another pointer is to try just to use 2 words. Truck_postsdaily isn't a username that you would want.

Do not make your username too long.

This one isn't a substantial deal, but if you can, try to choose a username that is short and to the point.

There's no need to stress about discovering the best username. You can always change it later on down the roadway by simply entering into your account settings. Likewise, if you're getting stuck looking for a readily available username, try taking a look at the account names of some of the bigger accounts in different specific niches. This will assist you create some concepts for your particular niche. Here's some examples to get you started:

- trucks_daily.
- truck_domination.
- trucklover.
- foodporn.
- fitness_mentor.
- yogapostsdaily.
- cooking_clips.

You get the idea. Simply try and ensure that the word individuals will be searching for is first.

If you can set up such account, just start advertising by posting ads and monetize your account.

(EXTRA)

CHAPTER TEN

50 Others Ways To Earn Online.

1. Online forum Posting:

One of the most convenient ways to generate income online, if you have a flair for talking, is by online forum posting.

A lot of webmasters have actually begun hiring individuals to post on their online forums so that their forums look busy and popular. They feel that by making their online forums look more popular, they will be able to bring in more long-term visitors.

When you're posting in online forums, all you would have to do is initiate brand-new threads, or react to existing ones, and keep discussions going. You might do this by posting fascinating thoughts, thought-provoking conversations, or mentor people things.

A cool perk of this job is that you get to learn brand-new things. Also, if you publish in online forums that you're already thinking about, you generally make money to have a good time. For you to become a forum poster, here are some actions you can take:

Check out freelancing websites such as Elance.com, Guru.com, Odesk.com, and so on. Look for online forum publishing jobs on those sites.

If you are called for an interview, respond back to the buyer on time.

Concur on the pay per post and the deadline.

Finish the job within the accepted due date.

Just how much can I get from forum posting?

For each forum post you make, the basic rates vary anywhere from $ 0.10 to $0.50 per post. If you have time to commit to this during the day and can make in between 200 to 1000 posts (depending on just how much your task is worth), then you can earn $100 a day. You can likewise, of course, do whatever you would like per day and then mix and match with another tip from our lists.

2. Forum Moderator:

As long as forums exist, forum moderators need to exist. This is because web designers need people to obstruct negative remarks, make sure things are running efficiently, and online forum users are getting their questions and remarks responded to.

To be an online forum mediator, you would require to monitor comments published by users, delete spam, response concerns from users, and reply to user messages. You would likewise motivate threads, add new material to the site, and block comments published by individuals who overlook forum rules.

This might be very intriguing for you to do if you have an interest in particular forums. Similar to forum publishing, you likewise have the potential to find out a lot.

You can find more tips here.

In order for you to end up being an online forum mediator, here are some steps you can take:

Post a profile on freelancing websites such as Elance.com, Guru.com, and Odesk.com. Describe your interests and your levels of knowledge.

Search for online forum moderator jobs on the very same freelancing websites, and obtain them. Google online forum small amounts of job openings.

If there are forums you're interested in, talk to the owner. A lot of individuals don't publish on freelancing sites but instead choose to employ individuals who publish a lot.

Just how much can I construct out of moderating online forums? Depending on your role and experience, you can make anywhere from $3 to $20 an hour.

3. Article writing:

You can make money by writing short articles for people with sites if you are a great writer.

Many site owners know that they require to keep their sites current and up to date, but don't have the time to develop brand-new material for them continuously. They employ people who can compose on their behalf since of that. For you to become a material writer, here are some actions you can take:.

Post a profile on freelancing websites such as Elance.com, Guru.com, and Odesk.com. Describe your interests and your levels of know-how.

Look for writing tasks on the exact same freelancing sites and make an application for them. Google author task openings. Ask the owners of sites that you already like if they are trying to find authors.

How much can I construct of writing?

Content writing tasks pay anywhere from $1 to $100+ based on the length of the short article and your competence. If you're currently an expert on the subject you're blogging about, you can typically charge a premium. Even if you are new to composing, you can make upwards of $.50 for each 100 words on an article.

4. Become A Blogger:

You can create a blog where you can talk about it if there's something you're passionate about. This is a fun way to share your passions while finding out and teaching about what you're currently delighted about. In order to do this well, you would require to be a great author with the capability to make people interested. You would also need to be able to publish fairly routinely to a blog site.

Blogs can be monetized in numerous methods. Simply some ways are to have companies pay you to post their ads (this is better for blog sites with a lot of traffic) or put Google AdSense on your blog site. With this alternative, Google pays you whenever somebody clicks on an ad.

In order for you to become a Blogger, here are some steps you can take:

Pick a business to blog with. Two of the most popular ones are Blogger or Wordpress.

Choose if you want a totally free account or if you would like to host the blog site on your own domain Most individuals choose to purchase a domain so that their blog site appears more professional. If you select to do this, you'll need to register with a hosting business (I suggest HostGator-- their strategies are as low as $4.95 a month), and then have your domain routed to the hosting company. This might sound hard, but it's very easy, and HostGator to r's consumer assistance can assist you with any questions.

After your blog is set up, embellish it nevertheless you would like (Wordpress calls the blog site skins "styles", and Blogger calls them "design templates"). Post news, lessons, stories, or anything relevant to your blog site. Include content as frequently as possible so that you develop a regular readership base Start advertising your site on socials media, amongst friends, or by means of other traffic methods (you can outsource a great deal of this to Burn Your To-Do List if you don't have the time or knowledge).

Just how much can I make out of blogging?

It can take a while to establish a blog site, but the profit potentials can be quite large. Some individuals report making in the countless dollars from a blog. Your earnings will differ based on the traffic you get to the blog, how intriguing your material is, how frequently you post, and the kinds of advertisements you place on your blog.

5. **Visitor Writer:**

Web designers sometimes require particular specialists to develop material for their websites. They may not know sufficient about a specific subject or wish to have somebody else's insight. If you're an expert in any specific niche, you can make some excellent cash by composing in and using your knowledge. In order for you to end up being a visitor author, here are some actions you can take:

Make certain to develop yourself as an expert in your specific niche by making a presence in the websites and online forums in your location of interest. Sometimes, people will simply ask if you're interested in creating material.

After you've developed an existence, you can likewise compose to site and forum owners and let them understand what your knowledge is, which you 'd have an interest in producing content for them need to be interested.

Make sure your content is composed and sent as early as possible when you get a composing job. If you develop an excellent track record, you can get references for other sites and hopefully wind up writing for more.

How much can I earn being a visitor writer?

Depending on the length of the piece you create and the obscurity of the subject, you can make anywhere from $25 to $200 each time you write.

6. Podcasting:

Podcasting is comparable to blogging; just you would do it via voice instead of typing. You would get the exact same benefits and approach it the very same way (post regular content, and so on) however, it's simply a method to fit individuals who would rather learn via reading versus listening.

To get going with podcasting, you require a headphone, microphone, and software in which to record your audio.

You can make money with podcasting the same method you would go with blogging-- via advertisements, Google AdSense, and by suggesting other programs that offer commissions.

For you to end up being a podcaster, here are some steps you can take: Produce a site with which to put podcasts on. If you don't already have something, tape your content-- you can utilize a totally free recording program such as Audacity. Transform your recordings to mp3. Submit your mp3 in addition to a description to your site. Start sharing it! Get it transformed in to MP3 format. Submit the mp3 on your site. Include content as regularly as possible so that you construct up a regular listener base.

Start marketing your website on social networks, amongst pals, or by means of other traffic techniques (you can outsource a great deal of this to Burn Your To-Do List if you do not have the time or knowhow).

7. Online Counselor:

Many individuals like to go online for therapy rather than meeting individuals face to face. They feel that they can be more anonymous this method, and they also have the convenience of not requiring to drive anywhere. If you can counsel people efficiently, this might be a fun job for you. You do not require to have a unique degree, although it would obviously provide you with a cutting edge.

For you to become an online therapist, here are some steps you can take: Develop a website that discusses your certifications and how you are able to help people. Let them understand if you don't have a degree or certifications to recommend anything to individuals. Some people just want to pay you so that you can listen to them, and they can vent their aggravations. Just make certain not to overstep what you can lawfully do.

Start advertising your site on social media networks, among good friends, or through other traffic methods (you can contract out a great deal of this to Burn Your To-Do List if you don't have the time or knowhow).

Start developing your consumer base. Do a fantastic job, execute word-of-mouth recommendation programs, and start collecting reviews from individuals you assist. Just how much can I construct of being an online counsellor?

Depending on your skill level, you can make from $100-$ 200 an hour and upwards.

8. Translation:

If you understand any other second language, then it will help you generate income by choosing translation jobs. This is another easy way to make use of your extra time and convert it into cash. If you understand any of the languages for which translators are in substantial need, specifically.

In order for you to end up being a Translator, here are some steps you can take:

You can get worked with for translation jobs through any of the freelancing sites. There are many websites that supply translation services specifically. You can submit your interest and get worked with through any of those sites Recognize the websites which publish all the jobs related to translation. Get yourself registered in those sites

You can begin your own site and make individuals learn about the translation services that you are ready to use. How much can I make money for translation tasks?

You can get paid anything from $0.01 per word depending upon the demand for the language. You can charge an excellent rate per word if the number of translators for the language is scarce. Are you thinking about serving as an agent or intermediary? Do you have a propensity for business and are excellent in handling people? Then noted below are some ideas that may fit you.

9. Outsourcing Middle-Man:

Lots of businesses want to employ people to assist them to broaden their web presence, developing content for their blog site, or help assist them with other jobs. If you are proficient at handling people along with marketing, you can act as an "agent" for some outsourcers.

Recognize people that can do certain work and then advertise their services to other businesses. Mark up the cost so that you can make a profit.

In order for you to end up being an outsourcing middle-man, here are some actions you can take: Check out freelancing websites, websites, and online forums to find people that you can work with. Create a website where you lay out the services your group can do, along with rates and turnaround times.

Start advertising your website on socials media, amongst pals, or via other traffic methods Start developing your client base. Do an excellent job, execute word-of-mouth recommendation programs, and start collecting reviews from individuals you help. Just how much can I make out of being an outsourcing middle-man?

A great deal of just how much you can make depends upon the type of services you use, how numerous customers you can handle at the same time, and how well you can market your services.

10. Worker Referral:

Numerous companies will offer referral bonuses for people who can hire exceptional new staff members for their organization. This can be a simple way to earn some additional money if you understand a lot of individuals or have relationships with employers. You can also discover potential prospects for business by using the internet. In order for you to end up being a staff member referrer, here are some actions you can take:

Most business do have worker recommendation programs, which suggests you have a great deal of chance to assist workers to find potential jobs. Offer them a call and ask if you're unsure if a business uses a referral program. You may want to begin with your own company if you currently work. If the people in your network are looking for tasks, discover out.

Go on freelancing websites like Elance.com, Guru.com, and Odesk.com, and take a look at the profiles of people there. Communicate with individuals that sound good, and see if they 'd have an interest in getting more regular work.

Refer individuals to HR of the company you deal with or other businesses that you're suggesting them for. If they get worked with, you will get paid. You can also try to build up a relationship with external employers. You can get a list of present job openings from them if you can do this. This can be exceptionally financially rewarding.

Just how much can I make out of being a staff member referrer?

Bonus offers are anywhere from $50 to the $1000's of dollars. A lot of this depends upon the kind of position (the more powerful the qualifications required, the greater the recommendation bonus) as well as the company you're working with.

11. Become a site or domain broker:

There is a lot of people thinking about purchasing individuals' websites. They wish to buy websites so that they can own established websites without needing to do the deal with their own, or they see earnings potential on sites, and so on, etc. A lot of individuals would love to sell their sites, too, however, do not know-how.

As a site broker, you can link purchasers and sellers to each other and take a portion of the sale for making the introductions. In order for you to end up being a website broker, here are some actions you can take:

Produce a website laying out the essentials of what you do. As you get sellers and purchasers interested, update the website with what buyers are looking for and what sellers have. Do not put seller's site information on your website; otherwise, buyers can walk around you to bypass your commission. Simply put necessary details.

Start discovering people thinking about buying or selling their sites. You can find these individuals by going on existing websites for buying and selling, such as Flippa.com, SiteSell.com, or BuySellWebsite.com. Even if individuals are currently noted on one website, it does not indicate they do not desire extra aid.

Do not offer website details to buyers till you get them to sign documents stating that they won't go around you, sign a non-compete, etc.

When a deal is made, collect a portion of the profits. Just how much can I make out of being a site broker?

You can make anywhere from $100 to the countless dollars, depending on how vital a website and domain is.

12. Start A Forum Posting Website:

As mentioned in the past, many web designers desire people to post in their forums. A lot of times, they will employ just someone, however, at other times, they desire a lot of individuals to go in at the same time, but don't seem like employing a lot of specific people.

If you can pool up 5-10 online forum posters yourself, you can offer a "one-stop" service where a web designer can pay you, and you can then head out and pay people individually. In order for you to start a forum publishing site, here are some steps you can take:

Find a website advertising your services.

You can hire online forum posters from any of the freelancing websites or by looking on forums where people are interested in working, such as work-at-home mommy websites.

How much can I construct out of having a forum posting business?

Certainly, a lot will depend on what you charge and how much you need to pay your employees, but you can quickly make $100/day by doing this after getting adequate customers.

13. Referral Exchange Programs:

Numerous independent developers take a lot of work from clients. There are times when they have excessive work to do and can't take on brand-new tasks, and so they have to hand down brand-new tasks.

You can create relationships with these people to take their excess work, and then either outsource it or do it yourself. On the other hand, if you have excessive work to handle. You can refer it to other individuals and charge them costs for your references.

No matter which method you choose to do this, you can benefit.

- In order for you to do a referral exchange, here are some actions you can take
- Get yourself registered in recommendation exchange forums

- Discover individuals that can take last-minute work
- Discover individuals that are in your market and frequently accepting freelance work
- Choose rates that you will pay individuals that offer you work, and rates you will charge for contracting out work
- Make sure to do an excellent task and just to refer individuals you trust so that you can continue doing this without the worry about harming your reputation.

How much money can I make out of recommendation exchange?

The revenues will alter based on how much you charge for referring work, as well as what you pay individuals for providing you referrals. You also need to represent how much you charge to do the real work. You can quickly make $100 a day doing this, though, once you build up your partner base.

14. Purchasing and selling links:

In order to get higher search engine rankings on Google, a lot of people feel that they need to have a lot of backlinks pointing their site.

Backlinks are links on other individuals' websites pointing to another website. When somebody links to another individual's website, it reveals Google that their site is worth connecting to, and so Google gives it a choice for their online search engine positionings. The higher the online search engine positioning, the more promotion a company gets, so a lot of people tries hard to get more links to their sites.

Because so numerous individuals desire links, you can benefit from this by functioning as an intermediary between individuals who want to offer links and people who are willing to buy them.

In order for you to buy and sell links, here are some actions you can take:

You can search for those who desire to purchase or offer links in forums of sites that discuss links

(Example: http://www.linkadage.com/).

Make yourself mindful of the link purchasing and selling standards.

Advertise only relevant links (links that have high Page Rank on Google). You can likewise develop a site advertising your services.

Start marketing your website on social media networks, amongst friends, or using other traffic techniques (you can contract out a lot of this to Burn Your To-Do List if you do not have the time or knowledge).

How much money can I construct of purchasing and selling links?

It depends on the quantity you charge for linking individuals. You can also buy links by yourself and after that charge individuals for them, in which you can develop your own pricing. You can make anywhere from $1 to $300 for a link, depending on how vital the website is.

15. Resell SSL Certificates:

An SSL certificate is something that sites typically utilize to show that their site is safe and secure. This certificate is digitally "signed" by a certificate authority that people currently trust after they confirm the determination of a reliable website.

Lots of website visitors require to understand a site is safe and secure before they submit payment or personal details, so web designers NEED the SSL certificates.

You can end up being a partner with any company that provides SSL certificates and resell them on their behalf. These businesses either will either offer their SSL certificates to you at a discount, and you can resell them, or they will use your incentives based upon the number of sales you make. You can find examples of such rewards here or here.

In order for you to end up being a partner to resell SSL certificates, here are some steps you can take: Browse the internet and make a list of companies that provide SSL certificates. Sign up for partnership account with the company. Determine potential clients and make the sales. Supply a list of number of sales you produced the month to the business. Take pleasure in the sales reward.

Just how much income can I make by reselling SSL certificates?

It depends on the number of certificates you sell and how much that specific company is offering if the business with which you have ended up being a partner offer sales rewards.

Your profit will be the margin that you keep for yourself if the business with which you have ended up being a partner offer certificates at affordable costs for you.

16. Drop Shipping:

Some people think twice to sell on eBay and other websites because they do not desire to have to go through the discomfort of keeping products, getting them appropriately packaged, and then delivering the items to clients. There is an alternative to that, though, called dropshipping. If you choose this, then you don't need to touch the products at all.

All you would do is sell the items, and then once you make a sale, a wholesaler would deliver it in your place as quickly as you supply them the name and address of each consumer. In order for you to do drop shipping, here are some actions you can take:

Get yourself registered in eBay as a seller and develop your own website

Make a list of wholesalers who supply drop shipping. Make sure the drop shippers do not include their contact information on the plans they send (otherwise, customers can go straight to them in the future). You can discover numerous dropshipping companies by going to this website.

Note the items that wholesalers can deliver, start marketing your site on social media networks, amongst buddies, or using other traffic techniques (you can contract out a great deal of this to Burn Your To-Do List if you don't have the time or knowhow).

Just how much money can I make from dropshipping?

The distinction between the list price and the wholesaler price will be the earnings margin that you will delight in. You can make anywhere from a couple of dollars to countless dollars per sale, depending upon what you're selling. You can certainly make $100 a day or more with this.

17. Sell your unused items:

If you have unused products or anything from old clothes to your grandmother's antiques in your home, then try to sell those products on eBay.

You've undoubtedly heard the saying, "One guy's trash is another male's treasure," and it could be rather possible to make a fair bit of money while uncluttering your house.

In order for you to sell your products, here are some actions you can take:

Get registered in eBay as a seller

Establish your own Paypal account to receive the payment. Browse your house and recognize the unused things that you wish to offer. List your products for sale on eBay

Just how much cash can I construct of selling unused items?

This depends on what you're selling, naturally. You can make anywhere from a few dollars to thousands of dollars by selling your unused items.

18. Buy and Sell Items on eBay:

You can try to purchase other people's products and sell them for a higher rate if you regular eBay. A lot of times people misspell their listings or do not rather know the worth of what they're selling, so you can score deals and then resell them for a profit. Another alternative is to buy items in bulk and offer them individually to various buyers at a higher rate.

You can do this either by putting an ad to attract those thinking about offering their unused products or check out eBay itself to buy and sell old products.

For you to purchase and offer other individuals' junk, here are some actions you can take:

• Go through eBay and see what items you can find.

- Purchase items which you believe will sell well
- Recognize buyers who want to acquire the products
- You might also desire to think about developing a website and marketing on locations other than eBay.

<u>How much cash can I make out of purchasing and offering junk?</u>

This will depend on the profit margins you produce and the worth of each product. You can make anywhere from a couple of dollars to a few hundred.

19. Offer other individuals items on eBay on their behalf:

On eBay you have an alternative to list items that are not yet in your belongings. However, if you select to do it, then you need to guarantee that you do not breach eBay's pre-sale product policy.

The cool aspect of this is that you can buy things online that are close to offering out, and after that, list them on eBay while you wait to get them.

You can also offer your good friend's items without requiring to have them in your home physically.

Another thing you can do is sell items before you purchase them to determine need. This is a cool method to get additional profit without needing to take on any risk.

Some things you can sell are tickets, In order to offer other people's scrap on eBay, here are some actions you can take:

- Get yourself registered in eBay and set up a payment technique to get the payment
- Set up a virtual shop as a purchaser
- Select a couple of items from others who want to offer their products and list them in your item page
- Recognize potential purchasers who would have an interest in buying the item

How much money can I make by offering other people's junk on eBay?

You can make anywhere from a couple of dollars to thousands of dollars by doing this.

20. Write an eBook on trading strategies in eBay:

If you decide to do the above mentioned items with success and are a skilled author, then why not write an eBook about using eBay to make a great deal of money?

Numerous individuals may be conscious of eBay fundamentals, and they might still buy the book to look out for new ways. Make the eBook as innovative and straightforward as possible. A well-advertised book can cost a long period, and any profit you make will be pure earnings as the product would be delivered digitally, and there would be no shipping costs. For you to write and offer an eBook, here are some steps you can take:

- When you get familiar with eBay, start writing an eBook describing how to use eBay and make money with it
- Try to keep the book as basic as possible to draw in more buyers
- Offer a memorable title to your eBook
- Market it for sale in eBay itself
- Get the sale done and delight in the profit
- Start marketing your book on social networks, among buddies, or by means of other traffic methods (you can contract out a great deal of this to Burn Your To-Do List if you don't have the time or knowhow).

Just how much money can I make by offering the eBook?

It depends on the price of the book. It depends upon the variety of books sold. It depends on the client feedback and evaluation for the eBook

Do you have a great deal of spare time? Are you interested in using it to make money? Do online tasks interest you? If so, some of the ideas noted below may fit you.

21. Take Part in Paid Surveys:

This is one of the methods that a lot of students love to make fast and simple cash. You get paid to get involved in studies as well as share your viewpoint when you work with paid studies. While these do not pay along with some other alternatives, the incomes build-up, and all work is really easy. In order for you to take part in Paid Surveys, here are some actions you can take:

- Identify legitimate paid survey sites
- Get signed up in a couple of websites, to begin with
- Let the company learn about the type of surveys you would be interested in taking part in
- Start taking part in as many surveys as possible
- Share your truthful opinion about the products
- Send back the completed study type at the earliest or within the due date
- You require a computer with an internet connection.
- You need to have a viewpoint concerning the item
- You should have some extra time to submit the study kind and send it back on time

How much can I make out of Paid Surveys?

You can make anything in between $1 and $100 depending on the kind of survey and the length of the study

Besides cash, you can likewise enjoy some freebies, discount coupons, lucky draw, etc

22. Take up part-time Data Entry tasks:

A lot of businesses have random requests for various things, such as transforming difficult copy data to electronic data.

If you have excellent keyboarding skills with terrific precision, then why not earn money out it?

For you to become a part-time Data Entry operator, here are some actions you can take:

Keep an eye out for data entry openings in freelancing sites such as Elance.com, Guru.com, and Odesk.com.

- Start looking for those jobs.
- Get the documents done on time.
- Do the job as properly as possible
- Send back the given job within needed due date
- Collect reviews and use rewards for people to refer their friends.

Just how much can I make out of Data Entry?

You can make anything between $1 and $5 per hour, depending on your speed and trouble of the task.

23. Get employed as Virtual Assistant:

People who run their own company mostly find it very hard to handle and organize things on their own.

By working as a virtual assistant, you can help people schedule meetings, arrange daily activities, response telephone call, etc., and so on.

You can choose to get hired as a virtual assistant if you are excellent at research and arranging things. In order for you to become a Virtual Assistant, here are some steps you can take:

Keep an eye out for virtual assistant openings in freelancing websites such as Elance.com, Guru.com, and Odesk.com

Start requesting those tasks

Search for as numerous clients as possible. Start marketing on social media networks, among good friends, or via other traffic methods (you can outsource a lot of this to Burn Your To-Do List if you do not have the time or knowhow).

How much can I make by functioning as a virtual assistant? You can make anywhere between $3 to upwards of $100 per hour, depending upon your capability and experience.

24. Participate in contests:

You can start getting involved in contests provided by different sites if you have a lot of time to extra.

It's likely that you will not win all of the contests, but the more you participate, the better your chances.

Little things do start earning up, and besides money, you can possibly win things like film tickets, sample items, present vouchers, etc. Where do I look for contests?

Search through the internet and make a list of sites which offer contests

Get registered in those sites and look for brand-new contests daily

Take part in as numerous contests as possible

Check out the search engines frequently and try to find any new contests

What do I gain by taking part in contests?

You can win money as well as other benefits like gift trips, cards, and discount coupons.

25. Modifying and Proofreading tasks:

There are times in which reports or posts need to be edited and proofread before they're all set to be published online. If you are a native speaker of whatever language a client needs a document proofread, or have excellent command over that language, then you can get editing and proofreading jobs. In order for you to acquire modifying and checking jobs, here are some actions you can take:

* Get yourself registered in all the freelancing websites such as Elance.com, Guru.com, and Odesk.com

- Get yourself registered to sites which provide editing/proofreading services to their clients
- Check task postings daily and use to ones that you are gotten approved for.
- Get hired and begin earning

How much can I construct of Editing/Proofreading jobs?

Lots of individuals see this as a very vital job and will spend on it. You can make money per short article or by the hour. If you opt for the latter route, expect at least $5 an hour for it, upwards to about $20 an hour.

26. Email And Phone handling:

This resembles a virtual assistant position, however, does not require making appointments or requiring any substantial skills. To do email and phone handling, you would mostly do things such as cold calling, answering questions over the phone, and managing e-mails.

Company owners typically tends to employ support staff to handle these tasks, as they're often too busy to do them themselves. This is one of the simple ways to earn extra income along with your regular earnings.

For you to acquire email and phone handling tasks, here are some steps you can take:

Obtain registered in all the freelancing websites like Elance.com, Guru.com, and Odesk.com

Check job posts to see what people are trying to find and make an application for the jobs that demand your skills

Just how much can I construct of Email/Phone handling jobs?

You can expect anything from $3 to $10 per hour depending upon your experience, and if there are any skills you need to learn about beforehand (at times - really seldom - you may need to understand complex topics).

27. Browse the internet and get paid:

It may sound a bit tough to believe, but you can earn money to browse the internet. They will typically pay you to keep it on while you are surfing the web if you set up a business's software application.

The reason the companies do this is so that they can track your activity and find out what sites their users go to, as well as find out how to market.

The downside of this one is that in some cases, you'll begin discovering random advertisements turning up, so do your due diligence and get a popup blocker (can be found free of charge by running a Google search). In order for you to browse the net and get paid, here are some actions you can take:

Search through the web and make a list of businesses that pay you to surf the web. Here's a listing from Yahoo that gives a great amount of companies. Download and install their tracking software application. Check out the internet and start earning. Just how much do I get paid?

Companies pay you something around $0.50 for an hour you browse and pay you something around $0.05 or $0.10 for every referral you supp

28. Click on advertisements and get paid:

Some companies will pay you to click on their ads in hopes of you liking the content on the other side. You can make money for each advertisement you click, and this requires no skills at all. Where do I find such a business?

Check out the internet and make a list of businesses that pay you to click on their ads (e.g. http://www.advercash.net/).

Ensure the site is a legitimate one before you get registered.

Get yourself signed up on the website.

Start clicking the ads and begin earning.

Just how much do I get paid?

You get paid something like $0.01 per click, as well as obtain cash for referring other individuals to the websites. You can make $100 a day on it, this one is planned to be one of the techniques that you use along with other ones to earn a total of $100 per day.

29. Check out freebie websites and get paid:

There are a lot of giveaway sites online that you can register to get a great deal of critical complementary products. While these sites do not always provide money, you can take the freebies and sell them to other individuals.

Where do I find such a business?

Browse through the web and make a list of companies that offer freebies. You can also go on forums such as MyCoupons or FatWallet to get concepts from there. Register for the offers you're interested in.

Just how much do I earn money?

Depending on the giveaways you get, you can offer them for anywhere from a dollar to $20 or so.

30. Take up online research work:

With brand-new services popping up every day, there is a constant requirement for web research and data collection.

This appears in many methods. Before somebody begins a new organization, they generally like to collect some fundamental data about the company: its demand and supply, its success, locations or nations where it can run well, and so on. Individuals that are searching for this are prepared to employ someone to gather such data and supply a report for them. If they ought to even start the company, they will utilize this report to decide.

There are other types of research study tasks readily available also, and this can be a fun method to find out about a lot of brand-new things.

The choice to begin with the company or not depends upon the outcomes of the research. Considering the requirement for the job, it is a great concept to use up online research study tasks if you are net savvy and have a great deal of time to spare. For you to earn money with online research work, here are some actions you can take:

- Apply for web research tasks.
- Do in-depth research and offer a report as needed by the purchaser.

Just how much cash can I make out of such research tasks?

If you work on repaired rate tasks, you can expect anything in between $5-$ 200 depending upon the trouble and the depth of the research study needed.

You can charge anything between $3 and $50 depending on your experience if you work on per hour tasks.

31. Offer online knowing videos:

In this web period, it appears as if everybody has an interest in gaining from home during their extra time. You can transform it into money by producing a step-by-step educational video if you are an expert in a specific area.

Try to make the video as basic and as simple as possible and begin selling it.

Simply remember that people only wish to buy quality content, so ensure that you're able to offer high-quality info that teaches people a lot.

In order for you to generate income selling training videos, here are some steps you can take: Start a site for yourself and begin publishing quality content to establish yourself as an expert.

Tape educational videos and upload them to your website.

Charge a fee to get the videos downloaded.

How much cash can I make?

You can charge a couple of dollars to a few hundred dollars per video, depending upon the details in the video and how readily available it is.

32. Offer Software review services:

Many developers are all set to spend for outdoor reviewers as they require sincere feedback about the programs they write.

If you are an expert in software advancement, then you can use truthful reviews for developers concerning their program or software application for a charge.

Make sure you supply an in-depth evaluation of both the good aspects and the defects when you provide such services.

You can charge a cost-based upon the need for your evaluation and your expertise in the area (Example: http://www.softwarejudge.com/,
http://philip.greenspun.com/software/design-review).

In order for you to earn money with software review services, here are some actions you can take:

- Compose a few software application evaluations free of charge to reveal individuals the quality of content that you can offer. Use these as samples.
- Look at software application forums and technique people who are developing brand-new programs.
- Do a Google search to discover prospective prospects.

Just how much cash can I make?

You can charge anywhere from $10 to thousands of dollars, depending upon your reputation and know-how. You could also consider having a company where lots of people do software application reviews. After that, you would develop one large detailed report with everyone's insight for a company. This might net you considerably more earnings.

33. Telecommuting tasks:

If you have an interest in working from home, then browse through the search engines and discover "Telecommuting jobs" (Example: http://www.tjobs.com/).

Identify the jobs which match your skill and begin making an application for it. If you get worked with, begin working from home and take pleasure in the cash. In order for you to generate income with telecommuting positions, here are some actions you can take:

- Search through the internet and try to find "Telecommuting jobs"
- Obtain registered on the websites which offer telecommuting tasks.
- Inspect the sites every day to discover tasks that ignite your interest and use for them.

Just how much money can I make?

These jobs usually pay anywhere from $3 to $50 an hour.

34. Send out greeting cards on others behalf for a cost:

Lots of people like to shock their buddies and loved ones by sending out an unforeseen greeting card.

Nevertheless, given that individuals are more pressed for time than ever now, the number of physical cards sent out has lowered, while the variety of digital cards has increased.

You can offer to send physical cards for people on their behalf so that they can still provide the fun gift of offering a physical, concrete card without needing to fret about going to the card shop and the post office.

Simply ask people for what kind of card they would like, and then the kind of message. You can handwrite the message in for a good homemade feel. You can buy the cards and mail them out on their behalf, spreading pleasure for everybody.

For you to generate income by sending welcoming cards, here are some actions you can take:

- Create a site for yourself.
- Tell your buddies and household about your brand-new services.
- Advertise in sites or forums, socials media, amongst good friends, or via other traffic techniques (you can contract out a great deal of this to Burn Your To-Do List if you do not have the time or knowhow).

How much cash can I make?

To make this worth your while, you truly need to get a lot of customers and do this wholesale. If you bought a $3 card and a stamp, you 'd make $2 if you charged $6 per card, xx. Undoubtedly the more you charge, the more you make. When you begin getting a lot of consumers, this can be financially rewarding and enjoyable for you.

35. Refer your good friends for Paid Surveys:

You currently know that you can generate income by filling out paid studies. You can also make money by referring people to those studies. In order for you to make money by referring your friends to paid surveys, here are some actions you can take:

- Search for recommendation scheme in the Paid Surveys sites that you get involved
- Refer your buddies to those sites
- Encourage your pals to complete the studies
- Get paid for those referrals

Just how much money can I get from recommendations?

You can get paid something around $1 or $2 for each recommendation you make

The rest of the entries are different methods that you can make cash online:

36. Start turning domains:

- Flipping domains resemble what individuals do in the property organization.
- You would purchase an inexpensive domain for $9 or $10.
- If you get a great domain, you can flip it at a website like DNForum or Flippa.

Some people will be prepared to pay a huge cost if the domain name is a keyword and apt rich for their niche (For example Business.com brought $7.5 million in 1999).

Though there aren't as, numerous domains offered as there used to be, but great ones still exist. A great deal of times, individuals may not have believed of certain domains themselves. However when they see them elsewhere, they recognize how valuable they are.

In order for you to earn money by buying and offering domains, here are some steps you can take:

You can purchase a domain from any of the domain sellers. My personal favourite is Namecheap (they make it really simple to send out domains to other individuals).

Make sure that the domains you purchase are either keyword-rich or otherwise extremely attractive.

Advertise your domain for sale in online forums like http://www.namepros.com/, http://www.dnforum.com/, and so on. How much cash can I construct of turning?

Your revenue can vary anything in between a few dollars to hundreds or thousands of dollars, depending on the domain you bought and the need for it.

37. Start turning sites:

Flipping sites is similar to turning domains. The distinction is that instead of right away turning around and offering a website, you can hang on to it, make some modifications, and after that sell it as an enhanced model. You can also hold on to it, make some cash from it, and after that, reveal possible buyers just how much it can make.

You can check out a fantastic article going into more information about this here. In order for you to earn money by purchasing and offering domains, here are some actions you can take:

- Browse websites like DNForum or Flippa to discover potential websites to purchase.
- You can also watch out for sites on Google, or come throughout websites while you're browsing, and start getting in touch with owners.

- After you've changed different things on the sites, go back to DNForum, Flippa, or individuals currently established in the site's niche to see if you might find buyers.

Just how much money can I construct of flipping?

People have made anywhere from $100 to millions of dollars with flipping. This is highly based on the revenue that your site makes.

38. Make money to check out emails:

There are lots of sites that pay you for reading emails. These are nothing, however, advertisement emails from a particular business.

You will be needed to open those emails and click the ad link supplied by the company to get paid. The business that pays you to make money by advertisers to show you their emails. The advertisers hope that when you click over, you'll wish to wind up buying whatever they're offering.

As they share your information with their marketers, they are paying a part of their ad profits with you. In order for you to earn money by checking out e-mails, here are some steps you can take:

Google "Get paid to check out emails."

Get registered in one or a lot of the sites that discuss this. (Some examples are http://www.getpaid5times.com/, http://wowearnings.com/, etc.)

Complete your individual information to finish the registration treatment

Open it and click on the link once you start receiving e-mails

Just how much money can I make out of checking out Emails? You can expect something around $0.10 per email

Aside from making money for reading e-mails, you can make money for referring your friends too

39. **Expert in something? Share your knowledge through your blog/website:**

Are you truly a specialist in any area? Then share your understanding through your blog site or website.

In order to get routine fans for your website, you can take a subject on which you are a specialist and detail one subject a day on the topic.

As soon as you construct traffic for your site, you can make a lot through marketing profits.

For you to generate income by sharing your understanding by means of a blog or site, here are some actions you can take:

- Start a site or blog on your own

- Get a fascinating subject on which you are a specialist.

- Choose up to one topic a day on the topic and share it with your users.

- One concept is to a training audio/video detailing it to step by step to keep it simple and interesting.

- Make the contents keyword rich to get more hits for your website.

- Develop traffic for your website and start making through advertisements.

- Promote in sites or forums, social networks, amongst good friends, or by means of other traffic techniques (you can outsource a lot of this to Burn Your To-Do List if you don't have the time or knowhow).

Just how much cash can I make?

It depends upon the traffic you construct and the number of advertisers you bring in. You can also attempt to generate income using affiliate deals.

Start writing newsletters and flow it to build a database:

If you're proficient at composing, a choice for you would be to produce newsletters and distribute them on a somewhat routine basis.

You can flow them totally free at first, but if your newsletters are truly fascinating and informative, you can develop up your subscriber base.

After that's done, you can charge to a "paid" model where individuals need to sign up to read your material, or you can just charge advertisers to promote themselves in your newsletter.

In order for you to make cash by composing a newsletter, here are some steps you can take:

- Pick a topic that you wish to write about
- Go to forums which deal with that particular topic
- Start taking part in those forums to establish yourself as a professional
- Develop a signup page for people to sign up for your newsletter.
- Circulate your newsletters on a specific regimen - either weekly, monthly, bimonthly, etc. As you construct up customers, contact marketers and let them know the number of people they would have access to if they chose to pay you for advertising.

Just how much money can I make?

This will depend upon your specific niche and quantity of subscribers, however, it would not be unreasonable to request $100 or more for an ad going out to 5,000 or more customers.

40. Sending Articles to Article Directories:

Sending articles to short article directory sites is among the very best methods for webmasters to construct traffic for their websites.

There are numerous short article directory sites on the web, however, lots of site owners only desire their posts sent to the top 25, 50, or 100.

As you can picture, it can take a long time to submit a post to numerous directories - especially if someone writes a lot of articles.

Since of this, web designers tend to hire people to send to post directory sites on their behalf. In order for you to become an Article Submitter, here are some steps you can take:

- Get yourself registered in freelancing sites such as Elance.com, Guru.com, and Odesk.com
- Search for short article submission tasks and start applying for them
- Start sending to required directory sites and maintain a log of where you have sent to and the username and password you used as soon as you get hired.
- Get the job finished on time and earn money.

How much money can I make?

You can earn in between $2 - $5 per hour, or earn a flat cost for every "x" submissions.

41. Connect Builder:

As we explained previously, backlinks are necessarily links on other individuals' websites pointing to another website. When somebody links to another person's website, it reveals Google that their website deserves connecting to; therefore Google offers it a preference for their search engine positionings.

The higher the search engine placement, the more publicity a service gets, so a lot of people attempt difficult to get more links to their websites.

There is a method to ethically "control" other websites to offering you links, and if you understand how to do that, then you can provide those services for a cost.

In order for you to become a link builder, here are some steps you can take:

- Get yourself registered in freelancing websites such as Elance.com, Guru.com, and Odesk.com
- Try to find link building tasks and begin making an application for them
- The purchaser will often provide you with places to develop links to. You would simply go to those places and follow

whatever guidelines the purchaser gives you (sometimes you have to create a profile, other times you need to make blog site comments, and so on).

- Start building quality links for your purchaser's site as soon as you get worked with.

How much cash can I make?

You can make anything between $2 - $8 per hour, depending on your know-how.

42. Find Expired Domains.

When somebody purchases a domain, they only purchase it for a particular time - generally 1, 2, 3, or 5 years.

If they forget to renew their domain or simply select not to, the domains enter into a database, and you can select to buy them. This is a cool method to profit from sites that currently have traffic.

Also, older domains usually get a higher choice in Google, so you can begin out with a website that has a good online search engine ranking. You can either build on these sites or turn them to other individuals for more money.

In order for you to generate income discovering ended domains, here are some steps you can take:

- Find an ended domain database. One example is right here.

- Buy domains.
- Decide whether you desire to enhance upon the websites, or just flip them. Make your modifications if you decide to enhance them.

Just how much can I make out of discovering expired domains?

The quantity of cash you can make would be various in each case. You could have a total loss (overall expense: $8.81 if you purchase a domain via Namecheap with a voucher code), or you might potentially make it into the thousands of dollars.

43. Transcription Jobs:

There are a lot of scenarios when things require to be transcribed. Some of these circumstances are when main meetings occur, or someone wishes to have a written version of a webinar or video.

Companies typically employ transcriptionists to type out whatever was stated since transcription can be quite prompt.

For you to become a transcriptionist, here are some actions you can take:.

Get yourself signed up on freelancing websites such as Elance.com, Guru.com, and Odesk.com.

Send them an e-mail to support@burnyourtodolist.com with what you can do, as they are always looking for more transcriptionists.

Get yourself signed up in the sites which offer transcription services exclusively (Example: http://www. way with words.eu/) and supply transcription services for their clients if employed. Look for transcription positions and begin obtaining them. Type up the audio when you get hired. Ensure it's error totally free.

Just how much can I make out of Transcription services?

You can make anything in between $3 - $50 per hour depending upon your speed, knowledge, and experience. Transcriptionists who can get things done faster have the ability to charge a premium.

44. End Up Being a Mystery Shopper:

Do you like to go shopping? Did you know that you can do it with other individuals' money?

Companies employ mystery consumers to collect info on numerous things like worker stability, cleanliness of the store, service provided, the method the staff members treats their customers, and so on. The business is in the requirement of such information to identify the problems and improve their services appropriately if needed.

Feel totally free to visit here or here if you desire to find out more. In order for you to end up being a Mystery Shopper, here are some actions you can take.

Look for "Mystery Shopper Jobs" in the web (Here is one example).

Get yourself signed up in freelancing sites such as Elance.com, Guru.com, and Odesk.com.

Try to find secret shopping jobs within the freelance websites.

Carry out the mystery shopping and make sure to fill out comprehensive reports with your experiences once you get worked with.

How much can I construct from such tasks?

Many locations pay anywhere from $5 to $10 an hour.

Provide online research assistance:

If you are an expert in any subject, begin offering online research aid throughout your extra time and generate income out of it.

There is a constant demand for online tutors who can provide research aid to students. In order for you to earn money with online research help, here are some actions you can take:

Check out the web for "online research assistance tasks" and begin requesting it.

Start your own website and note down the subjects for which you supply research assistance.

Promote in online forums or sites, socials media, among good friends, or through other traffic techniques (you can contract out a great deal of this to Burn Your To-Do List if you don't have the time or knowhow).

You may desire to consider putting your offer on a bulletin board system at a neighbouring school.

After getting clients, supply exceptional service so you can get more word of mouth recommendation clients.

Just how much cash can I construct such jobs?

You can charge anywhere from $3 to $50 per hour depending on your experience and expertise on the subject. Many people charge in between $10-$ 20.

45. Play online video games and make cash:

Some sites will pay you real money for the points you obtain in different games. To associate with major gaming for money, make certain that you have the appropriate graphics card, an upgraded CPU, joystick, and whatever else may be required for the specific video game you wish to play.

To understand more about playing video games for earning money, please refer here.

In order for you to generate income with online homework aid, here are some actions you can take:

- Run a Google look for "make cash to play video games". You'll find a couple of sites, including Gamesville, and PlayForMoney.
- How much money can I construct out of such tasks?
- The amount you earn will depend upon the type of game you play. You normally earn a little at a time, however once again, if you do this simultaneously with other methods in this book, it can be a great way to get relaxation and earn at the exact same time.
- Develop one website and sell it to great deals of people in the specific niche.
- You can develop one main design template and sell it to individuals in the very same industry if you are great at site style.
- You can produce a design template for hairdressers, contact all the hairstylists you know, and then offer them the website you created.

All you need to do to alter up the template is to alter the logo, company name, icons, etc. In order for you to make money with this, here are some steps you can take.

Design a remarkable site on your own. Include your portfolio and client testimonials.

Market your templates by promoting it in numerous sites. Market in sites or forums, socials media, amongst friends, or by means of other traffic techniques.

Cold call individuals in the industry that you want to offer websites to. People who don't have sites yet would be a prime market for this.

How much cash can I make?

You can fairly expect between $50 and $250 for each website you create.

46. Pay per click Arbitrage:

PPC arbitrage is when you buy ads on Google AdWords, and after that, when users click on the advertisements, they simply see a bunch of advertisements to go to other websites.

They click those advertisements, and you earn earnings.

The distinction in between the amount you pay to purchase the quantity and the advertisement you get per click is the revenue you make.

To know more about PPC arbitrage, do not hesitate to refer here.

For you to make cash with arbitrage services, here are some actions you can take:

Establish a very easy site on your own. You will use this to direct people to brand-new pages.

Purchase some PPC ads on Google AdWords.

Set up Google Adwords so that people are rerouted to your web page after they click through the advertisement.

Earn money for every single click on your ads

Pocket the difference

How much cash can I make?

This is extremely depending on a number of factors - the niche you're in, the number of advertisements you have up, just how much you're spending for each advertisement, how much you make money when individuals click on your advertisements, and so on. But you can securely assume anywhere from $.01 to $1. The secret with this is to scale to a significant degree.

47. Ecurrency Trading:

Ecurrency trading resembles stock trading, and simply like with stock trading, it's one of the riskier methods to make money - unless you are well conscious of what you are doing.

However, as soon as you get knowledgeable about it and understand when to buy or sell currencies, then you can make a great deal of revenue out of it.

Feel free to learn more here to find out more.

In order for you to generate income with ecurrency trading, here are some actions you can take:

Analyze the current market before you offer any currency or buy

Keep seeing the market to purchase or sell currencies at the correct time

If required, take suggestions from professionals in the area

How much cash can I make?

It depends on the currencies you hold and the decisions you make. This can be very lucrative, though, of course, it can also be a significant loss for you.

48. Expert in something? Earn money by ending up being a guide in about.com:

If you are a professional in any subject, then you can turn into one of the guides in about.com.

To end up being a guide in about.com, you require to check out their readily available topics and request the topics that you are a professional in.

You will need to go through their filtering procedure before getting hired, and then if they pick you as one of the guides, you need to undergo their online training.

You can discover more about this by going here.

Just how much money can I make by ending up being an about.com guide?

Straight from the website: "In addition to a base payment (ensured to be $ 675 monthly for Guides in their first two years, with a minimum of $500 per month afterward), About.com pays Guides by determining pageview growth (month-over-month for Guides in their first year, and year-over-year every year after) with payment rewards for pageview growth. If your page views grow, you will never ever make less than $675 per month."

This is an excellent way to get money in addition to utilizing the other methods we have actually discussed.

Is your website effective? Make it a membership site:

Consider making it a subscription website if you have managed to build adequate traffic for your website.

A subscription website is one in which people need to pay in order to see the material on it.

This will only work if you have a strong follower base considering that countless websites have free material; however, it is certainly something to consider. In order for you to generate income with a membership website, here are some actions you can take:

- Select a niche on your own and begin a website
- Keep composing intriguing content within the niche you have selected

- Get involved in user forums which discusses your specific niche
- Build your trustworthiness by releasing only quality material
- Keep posting contents on a daily basis as long as possible
- Over some time, you can develop routine fans for your website
- After that is done, you can convert your site into a membership site and start earning

How much can I construct out of it?

You can play around with the numbers; however, even $5 or $10 a month adds up extremely rapidly.

49. Evaluation sites for a cost:

If you have a popular site with lots of traffic, you can begin evaluating websites in your specific niche for a charge.

A lot of people would love to utilize your traffic and would be more than happy to pay you to provide more direct exposure.

If you do this, make sure to supply honest and extensive evaluations about both the great elements and the defects. This is also a great way to get products for free.: -RRB-. In order for you to earn money by evaluating sites, here are some actions you can take.

Post an advertisement on your website stating that you are taking new customers for evaluations. That alone could be enough if your site is popular.

Do a search on Google and approach the sites in your specific niche. Sites that aren't high in the online search engine might be eager to get more traffic, and sites that already are high might still want more. The more offers you send, the better your results. Make certain to mention your website traffic numbers if you decide to send out e-mails.

How much can I construct it?

This will depend on how much traffic you get and what your specific niche is in. You can charge anywhere from $50 to $500 for each evaluation you do.

50. Expert services:

As an extension to website review services, once you acquire adequate experience and competence in examining websites and blogs, you can start an "upgrade" service by offering professional reports to sites. You can evaluate their sites and let them understand what needs to be repaired, what has worked the best for other sites, and what you think can be surpassed.

In order for you to earn money with expert services, here are some steps you can take:

- Post an advertisement on your website stating that you are taking brand-new customers for evaluations. That alone might be enough if your website is popular.

- Contact your old clients and let them know you're providing personal reviews that don't need to be posted for all of the general public to see.

- Do a search on Google and approach the sites in your niche. Websites that aren't high in the search engines may be excited to get more traffic, and sites that already are high may still desire more: the more offers you send out, the better your outcomes. Make sure to discuss your website traffic numbers if you choose to send out emails.

Just how much cash can I make?

You can charge from $100 per review and upwards.

CHAPTER ELEVEN

The 8 Myths About Creating Wealth.

You have most likely checked out or found out about various myths surrounding wealth and rich people, all of which prevent your mission for monetary self-reliance. Here are the most typical and most harmful

Misconception No. 1: How much you earn depends on how difficult you work. If this were real, then the physical, blue-collar employees, who have been striving for many years, would have been the most affluent individuals in the world. Naturally, this isn't real. They form most of the workforce and the huge majority of the middle-class. If you witnessed your parents coming home tired from a long day's operate in your youth, you probably found out that cash wasn't enough benefit for all that effort. Individuals who work" just" for the cash frequently have financial obligations because they comfort themselves with whatever they can purchase, stunning things they lack when working.

Misconception No. 2: Being paid for something you enjoy isn't work, and you shouldn't ask for money for doing something that is satisfying. Examine this with millionaires. They all have a lot of money that they do not need to work any longer. However, they work for other reasons, difficulty, fulfilment, the fullness of life, activity, fun and all are connected to a love for their work. They would do something else that would make them much happier, and that enables them to understand dreams if there was no delight in doing a particular task. If you do not enjoy your work, you will never become rich doing it! However, even if you enjoy your work does not indicate you should not earn money for it that is the ultimate objective, to get paid for what you currently delight in so it never feels like you are at work!

Misconception No. 3: You require to be in the ideal line of work to get wealth. Do you think so? This must indicate that all the individuals who are included in the same company are millionaires. This isn't real. In each business there are losers and winners; winners are plentiful, even in services that consist of horrible (too many) or" impossible" works like sweeping the streets, gathering the garbage, working in a factory, pumping gas, selling newspapers, etc. On the other hand, there are just as numerous "losers" in companies like offering realty, the management, or being a stockbroker.

Misconception No. 4: You need the ideal education to succeed

Are the most educated individuals truly the most affluent? Not at all! In this case, university teachers would be the wealthiest people on earth. Ask them about their wages if you get the opportunity. The fact is significantly different - the most affluent people are those who can convert their knowledge (or education) into cash, in the very best possible way. They can be extremely educated individuals (like creators, researchers, etc.) or almost oblivious.

Being formally uneducated does not relate to poor performance on the task or the failure to form a strong enough vision to bring an individual to success - they can easily be specialists without having a formal education.

Misconception No. 5: It utilized to be easier

Stats reveal an increase in the variety of millionaires worldwide every year. Discussing the "good old times" only uses convenience and a practical reason. If you look around, you'll see some individuals behaved the exact same method in the "excellent old times" as they do now, yet their success has actually been current. With technology and development come new ideas, needs and desires, and there are more business opportunities appearing daily to serve them.

Misconception No. 6: I'm too old (young).

You'll see that this isn't true at all if you investigate the life stories of some of the most successful people. Some became rich early in their lives (possibly from the stock market), while others found their fortune in their ageing. Ray Kroc, was more than fifty years old when he purchased and made the first McDonald's.

Misconception No. 7: I do not have sufficient cash to begin. You have to spend money to earn money.

This is no various from any other reason or "misconception." Like the others, it's apparent this one isn't real either. Lots of having made their fortunes going back to square one, living in a house or working out of their garage and yet they developed company empires that deserve billions of dollars today. The other components of success are far more important than having seed money to start a business. Yes, frequently cash assists, and it certainly doesn't harm. Like whatever else talked about in other misconceptions: it most likely assists, however, it is not constantly essential.

Misconception No. 8: I'll start when I understand whatever.

Success and acquiring wealth is a dynamic procedure. Some millionaires have actually even enabled themselves to go insolvent and then(even much faster) recreated their wealth, in some cases even higher than previously. Money itself isn't the barrier that is keeping you from being rich. No one can ever give you higher potential than your heart currently holds you need only discover its contents to find the one true path real your success in life. 6 Ways of Thinking" Rich". Abundant people have a method of thinking that is various from poor and middle-class people.

Let's take a look at six essential differences in between how rich individuals believe and how poor or middle-class individuals think. In this way, you can catch yourself believing as bad individuals do and rapidly switch over to how rich individuals think.

Yet, that's exactly how many people play the cash video game. Their primary concern is survival and security, not wealth and abundance. What is your objective? What is your real objective? What is your true intention? Abundant individuals' huge objective is to have huge wealth and abundance. Poor people's big objective is to have "enough to foot the bill ..." on time would be a wonder! Again, let me advise you of the power of intention. When your objective is to have enough to pay the bills, that's precisely just how much you'll get; just enough to foot the bill and generally not a cent more. You get what

you truly intend to get. If you desire to get abundant, your goal needs to be "rich." Not just enough to foot the bill and not simply enough to be comfy. Rich! Poor people are uncommitted to being rich. The majority of us have great reasons as to why it would be fantastic to be abundant, however what about the other side of the coin?

Exist factors why it might not be so excellent to be rich or go through the procedure of trying to get abundant? Each of us has a file on wealth in our mind. This file includes our individual beliefs that consist of why being wealthy would be excellent. For numerous individuals, their file likewise includes information as to why being abundant may not be so great.

These people have blended internal messages around cash and particularly wealth. One part of them says," Having more money will make life a lot more fun." However then another part screams," Yeah, but" I'm going to need to work like a dog! What kind of enjoyable is that?" One part says," I'll have the ability to travel the world." The other part responds," Yeah, and everybody in the world will want something from me." These blended messages are one of the greatest reasons that many people never prosper.

The # 1 reason most people do not get what they desire is they do not know what they desire. Abundant people are totally clear; they want wealth. They are unwavering in their desire. They are completely devoted to producing wealth. They will do "whatever it takes "to have wealth as long as it's ethical, legal and ethical. Rich individuals do not send combined messages to the universe. Poor people do. If you are not totally committed to creating wealth, chances are you won't Opportunities

Poor individuals believe small. In my company, some trainers delight in speaking to groups of 20. Others are comfortable with 100, others like an audience of 500, still others want 5000 people or more in participation. How do you desire to live your life? Will you play huge or play small? It's your choice.

But hear this. It's not about you. It's about living your mission. It's about living real to your function. It's about including your piece of the puzzle to the world. It's about serving others.

Most of us are so stuck in our egos that everything focuses on "me, me and more me." But again, it's not about you. It's about including worth to other individuals' lives. It's your choice. One roadway results in being broke and miserable, the other results in significance, money, and satisfaction.

It's time to stop hiding and begin marching. It's time to stop needing and start leading. It's time to start being the star that you are. It's time to share your gifts and value in a BIG method.

There could be thousands or even countless people depending on you. Are you approximately the challenge for our society and our children's sake? Let's hope so. Poor individuals are smaller sized than their problems. Getting abundant is not a stroll in the park.

It's a journey that is full of obstacles, detours, and twists. The simple truth is, success is messy. The road is laden with mistakes, and that's why many people do not take it. They do not want the inconveniences, the headaches and the obligations. Simply put, they do not desire the problems. Therein lies one of the biggest distinctions between rich people and poor people. Rich and successful individuals are bigger than their problems while poor and not successful people are smaller sized than their problems. Poor people will do nearly anything to prevent anything that appears like it could be a problem. They get away from challenges. The irony is that in their mission to make certain they do not have issues, they have the biggest problem of all, they're broke and miserable. The trick to success is not to try to avoid or diminish your problems; it's to grow yourself, so you're larger than any problem. Imagine a" level 2 "character individual taking a look at a" level 5" issue. Would this problem appear to be big or little? The answer is that from a "level 2" viewpoint, a "level 5" problem would appear BIG. Now think of a" level 8" individual looking at the exact same "level 5" issue. From this person's perspective, is this issue little or big? Magically the identical problem is now a small issue. And for a" level 10" individual, it's NO issue at all. It's just a daily event, like getting dressed or brushing your teeth. Whether you are poor or abundant, playing huge or playing small, issues do not go away. If you're breathing, you will constantly have so-called "issues". What's essential to recognize is that the size of the problem is never the real problem. What matters is the size of you! Remember, your wealth can only grow to the degree that you do! As soon as you have it, the idea is to grow yourself to a place where you can conquer any problems that get in your way of creating wealth and keeping it. Rich people do not back away from issues, do not prevent problems and do not complain about problems. Abundant individuals are financial warriors, and when a warrior is confronted with a difficulty they scream: Poor people concentrate on problems. Abundant individuals see potential growth. Poor individuals see a prospective loss. Abundant individuals concentrate o the rewards. Poor individuals concentrate on the dangers. It's the olden concern, is the glass half empty or half complete? We're not simply

145

speaking about "positive thinking" here, we're talking about a regular way of seeing the world. Poor people come from fear.

Their minds are constantly scanning for what's wrong or what could fail in any scenario. Their primary mindset is "What if it does not work?" or, more bluntly, "It won't work".

Rich people, as we discussed earlier, take obligation for developing their life and originate from the state of mind. It will work since I'll make it work. In the financial world, as in a lot of other areas, the threat is straight proportional to reward; generally, the greater the reward, the greater the threat. Individuals with rich mentalities are ready to take that danger. Rich individuals anticipate succeeding. They believe in their capabilities, they have confidence in their imagination, and they believe that must the "doo-doo hit the fan" , they can always make their refund or succeed in another method.

On the other hand, poor individuals anticipate stopping working. They do not have self-confidence in themselves and in their abilities, and ought to things not exercise, they think it would be devastating. You have to do something, purchase something, or start something to succeed financially. You have to see opportunities for profit all around you rather of concentrating on methods of losing cash.

CHAPTER TWELVE

Harness Your Mind to Create Prosperity

We now understand beyond a doubt that everything in the known universe, from the "physical" world to our innermost ideas is energy in movement.

Really our inner "psychological" reality and the world's "external" truth are an inter-woven quantum occasion. We are participants in a vibrant and open living universe. And we are, in fact living in two side-by-side overlapping worlds.

Sound weird?

Maybe. But if you see your thoughts and memories as "energy base" that exchange energy backwards and forward with the "external" physical world. You're right in line with modern quantum physics and neuroscience.

How Do We Create "Reality"

Today's PET diagnosis enables us to "see" the brain actively grow and alter with each thought. The power of an idea can no longer be excused lightly as an "esoteric theory". Each image of the "outdoors world" kinds and modifications of your brain to a physical level. From these pictures, our minds now construct what we call "truth" : Our eyes don't actually "see" anything. They merely collect packets of light being reflected off an object. Those packages of light are transferred into the brain as electronic signals. As regards to your past life, your brain then analyzes the signals and tells you what you are "seeing." Scientists are now stating what mystics have claimed for centuries, that life is an illusion. The "illusion" is that the world you view beyond yourself is the world as it really exists. After all, according to science, the "genuine world" is comprised of nothing more than vibrating energy. We now know that everyone produces their version of the world based on their beliefs, expectations, and previous history. "So how does all of this related to producing success?" you ask. Just this: Your interpretation of "success" is closely affected by what you envision, visualize, want or fear and turn down. Go into the Mind.

Let's have a look at what "success" truly is. Viewed in ways of Neuroscience, prosperity is a" psychological idea "housed in our physical brain. The "idea" of prosperity lives in the mindful rational portion of your brain. I'm sure you can provide a precise meaning of the word "prosperity" without becoming mentally involved. But when I ask you, "What does success mean to YOU personally" , whatever suddenly modifications.

In a millisecond, your subconscious mind briefly reviews your 2nd-grade buddy comparing their family's brand-new Cadillac to your family's Ford, or perhaps when you want-ed a brand-new bike, but were told to" be sensible" about your family's monetary status. Or told you would never "be flourishing" without ending up being a physician or lawyer. Where does this happen? Deep in your subconscious mind. And regrettably, the subconscious mind does NOT respond to "sensible reasoning" about how those old "lessons" no longer apply.

Does your lifestyle fall brief of your dreams? You can be sure that your subconscious mind is the basis of what holds you back! And the problem is each time you "review" one of those subconscious restricting thoughts, the neural tracts causing it are physically reinforced! This is not a theory. This is hard, observable science! You're going to have a neuron reprogramming (nerve cells brain cells) on a physical level. Your Brain is Growing or diminishing. We now discover that the brain is not unchanging organ we changeless thought it as soon as. Utilizing the forces of your mind to produce your perfect lifestyle can be a genuinely exhilarating experience. Produce a Million Dollar Stream of Income With Your Mind Now! My point for digging this up was to point out to you how you are now focusing on your mind about that event. Go ahead and pimp your mind about would you buy right now when you have a million dollars raw, hard cash. That is right; you might be thinking of a brand-new car, boat, mansion, toy, helping others, being economically complimentary, and perhaps you are even thinking of a vacation or journey to Hawall or other trips you would take. Now stop meditating on that and listen to learn how you can not simply "think" about it, however actually develop it in your life instantly!

Your mind accessed the very same thoughts, sensations, and sounds that you had at that time in your life. You might have felt somewhat mad or upset when you remembered it. Then, if you thought about having your own million dollars, what took place? If you really could imagine it in your mind, you really did think of what you would do with it, you probably even could see yourself living a "different life" than what you are living today. Did you do it? Did you experience it? I did. If you didn't, start from the beginning and do read it again - and this time, try to see it in your mind and truthfully consider what you would finish with your own million dollars.

The truth is that our minds are more powerful than we understand. As human beings, we can literally take something from our past and relive it over and over and over once again. You might understand somebody who does this.

Think about it. Have you ever heard somebody say almost the same thing when some-thing fails? Perhaps they say "I had a bad childhood", or "I'm no excellent at X", or some other negative statement that they have actually positioned upon themselves.

Without going into scientific information, you can find out to master your mind and use its creative/remembering ability to bring into your life whatever you desire. Particularly, you can alter your mind, so you create, not just abundance in every kind, however, you can really create a Million Dollar Income Stream into your life now.

How? By utilizing the very same tools that others utilize to bring themselves down into despair and develop poverty, you can utilize those tools in brand-new manner ins, which bring you up into happi-ness and success and create a Million Dollar Income ocean now. Exactly as you imagine about what you would do with the millions of dollars, if you do the following workouts every day, you will develop Million Dollar Income Streams in your life. It WILL happen quickly, easily, and completely natural as you rely on the power of your mind to create what you desire.-

Keep in mind what i am about to share with you are the exact steps to guarantee your

Money making secrets of mind power masters success. These are secrets. They have been hidden from the basic population for a factor. Now that they will be revealed to you, please honour them and take them seriously. This is essential. Despite the fact that I understand thousands (if not millions) of people will eventually read this product, only a choose few will really execute it. Why? Since even though the Million Dollar Income Stream will stream into your life easily and naturally, it does need some effort on your part- only. After you establish the system(in your mind), it will be entirely natural and effortless.

151

I invite you to be among the few who will use this invaluable information. Do what requires to be done at first and after that, enjoy the rewards for the rest of your life. Now, these are the exact steps to produce a Permanent Million Dollar Income Stream in your life now. You need first to eliminate all doubt from your being. Remove all hate, eliminate all sadness, get rid of all excuses.

You should BELIEVE that this will work for you since it will. So, step one: have faith that as you do this, it will work. Think that it will work for you, and it will. You need to take only 15 minutes a day to be on your own(alone) to perform the millionaire exercise. I do not care if you need to go into your closet or bathroom and lock the door- but you should do it. Do not question it; just do it.

You must close your eyes and duplicate the following verbatim(word for word), preferably out-loud for the entire 15 minutes. Every minute of every day, millions of dollars flow to me now instantly, easily, naturally now. You should repeat that declaration over and over and over once again in a rhythmic manner for a minimum of 15 minutes of every day for a two-month duration. After the 2 month period of doing that every day, you need to set a goal of precisely what quantity of cash you wish to have. For example, if you desire $1,468,920.00, you need to start using this quantity in your declarations. One million, four hundred sixty-eight thousand, nine hundred twenty dollars streams to me now, immediately, easily, naturally now. Do this for the next three months. During these next 3 months, after you are done duplicating the phrase, you should believe about either having that specific amount of cash in your checking account(visualize yourself taking a look at your bank statement with that exact quantity of money on your declaration). Then, I feel great about your accomplishment. Circumstances and situations will start emerging in your life that will enable this specific total up to manifest itself into your life. Simply be positive(remember you can not doubt, for if you do -you will not get the cash) and allow deep space to work its magic in your life. Step eight: Repeat actions one through seven. By doing so, you will obtain a lot of Dollar Income Streams in your life.

You now have the exact steps.

Remember to use them.

Thank you for allowing me to share these secret steps with you.

I want you to complete success as you create your own Million Empire now.

CHAPTER THIRTEEN

Cash As An Illusion, a Shadow of Something Else

The very essential step to having wealth is to understand what it is. And few individuals understand what it is, in and of itself. What is wealth? What triggers it? What triggers the cause of it? Let us begin with money, the world's sign of wealth, and then move deeper. Money is not genuine. Cash is merely legal tender, a form of exchange. We utilize it to exchange value.

It represents value. Cash is the "body" of worth. It is the physical representation of value that fluctuates in ourselves, within us. Not within" things" outside of us, but within us. For without us, what can the value of a thing, such as a vehicle, be to us? Nothing, at least not to us.

Simply put, it is we, the observers, that location worth crazes; however, this worth is true value in us- we offer worth to the product things. The material things have no" cash" worth in themselves -we give that to them. So, cash is the external physical representation of a specific section of our internal value, within us, within you. That is why a home or a block of shares valued at $1 million today can be up to a valuation of half a million dollars tomorrow when fear is presented into the hearts of those involved. The fear eliminates a part of the internal worths of the participants, which is reflected by the paper cash, the" body" of value. Here is something else: physical fiat money does not even represent money completely. It can not reasonably do that. By some quotes (and this varies from country to nation), just as little as 4% of the cash in the banks exists as paper money. Think of how much cotton, linen, pulp, and metal the world would require so regarding making all the cash every-one has in his/her checking account. Envision how much area it would require to keep all this cash in paper kind. If you were to stack just one million US$ 1 bills, it would weigh one lot and be 361 feet high. Neither does money exist as gold reserves anymore. This is for precisely the exact same factor- we lacked the affordable ability to keep a gold standard in the 1970s.

What does it exist as the money that we are constantly talking about? It is all just numbers written on paper and computer system storage devices, and assigned to people and entities such as business and financial investments, or more properly, additional records! The last time people stopped believing in it in a large adequate extent was just before the Depression when big numbers of people rushed to their banks to withdraw their money and discovered that they might not all get it.

So, cash is not real - something else is. Money is simply the shadow of that other something. The initial step to wealth is to understand what money truly is, or more accurately, what it represents. Learn not to take a look at the cash many of the time. As you will soon see, it is really rare in a day that you ought to ever look at cash as you understand it today - the money, the savings account, the expenses, etc. This is simply the shadow and not the genuine thing. Looking at the shadow, the physical money, as you will soon see, is the majority of the time extremely unwise and unhealthy for you and your finances.

Look, instead, at the worth within you and within people, and the flowing and exchanging of this value in between people. Our internal value is what creates money. Money is the shadow of our internal worth. Establish this internal worth in yourself and in others and your external cash and wealth will similarly increase immediately, without stop working.

Know this nevertheless: Money represents an aspect of an individual's internal worth; however, that does not imply that it represents an individual's whole internal worth. That is extremely important. It is not about self-worth. Money just represents an element of that internal value that refers to wealth. You can not for that reason say that a rich person has a greater self-respect and worth than a poor individual, but you can properly say that in matters that relate and pertain to money, the wealthy person has a higher internal worth because aspect of worth or that the individual chooses to exercise a higher percentage of this internal value. This section of internal value that assesses the outdoors as money, when worked out, is called Wealth Consciousness. It is available to all people similarly and can be established by and within all individuals equally. Like everything else that is essential to our being alive, such as air, wealth awareness is free to all. However, you can choose to establish it or not develop it, or to exercise it or not. At any time, you can alter your choice, and nothing beyond you can stop you. You require absolutely nothing beyond yourself to increase your wealth consciousness and for that reason, your cash. All you require is within you right now. You might have forgotten it. However, it is right there. You will now remember it. And the primary step to that is to keep in mind that money is not genuine constantly; it is the shadow of something else. And here is another secret: Wealth awareness is just the expansion of your consciousness and awareness into the rich parts of your Self. That is why all that you need to increase your wealth consciousness is within you currently. You are already rich; however, you have been taught to select not to experience your wealth. This insight modifications whatever. Like the rich individuals, you can now understand how to and select to begin experiencing the wealthy you. You have more wealth capability within you than you can perhaps experience in a life-time. Because of any condition, you need not fret that you have reached your limit of ending up being wealthy in any way or. Neither do you require to know how to convert wealth consciousness into paper money -as you will see, it will take place immediately. All you require to do is expand your wealth awareness and exercise it, act on it, be it, and the circumstances and chances for the comparable conversion into money will

157

present themselves automatically to you. None of the incredibly wealthy individuals today could have, at the time when they were not wealthy, possibly forecasted and prepared the specific sequence of events that would lead to their tremendous wealth. They most likely had a set of objectives and a plan. However, any among them will tell you that they fulfilled many "coincidences" and chances that signed up with the dots for them in ways they might never ever have predicted. Their goals were their own doing, the paths that led to them entering being, and exceeding them, were remarkably smart yet unforeseen. You will now see how to make them occur in your life- you may not have the ability to anticipate their sequence; however you can make these "fortunate coincidences" happen to you every day of your life. By the way, it is not only fiat money that is not genuine. A lot of the important things around you that you hold so genuine are not real at all either. You will start a beautiful, empowering and liberating journey

that will show you precisely what your world is in a manner in which you have actually never looked at it before. It is a journey that will open your eyes and free your wings. You are about to look "under the hood" of the Life, you are about to learn how to personalize your world to your liking. You are about to attain Wealth Consciousness. As soon as you do, avoiding success and wealth will become very hard. Yes, you read that properly. It will be really difficult for you not to have success and wealth when you have wealth consciousness. Success and wealth will follow you instantly anywhere you go. You will not need to concern yourself with their quest, yet they will discover you. You will be complimentary to experience other elements of life that you might not have even dreamt of before, dimensions of Self and Life that are amazing. The same chooses joy, for you will see it here in this book also. GOD BLESS YOUR LIFE!

www.ingramcontent.com/pod-product-compliance
Lightning Source LLC
Chambersburg PA
CBHW021412210526
45463CB00001B/336